Better Homes and Gardens

ALL-TIME FAVORITE

Beef recipes

On the cover: Impress special guests with a *Boneless Rib Roast* (see roasting chart, page 13) garnished with *Crumb-Topped Tomatoes* (see recipe, page 23). Or stretch the budget with *Cider Stew* (see recipe, page 72). Vary the grilled hamburger menu with *Taco Salad* (see recipe, page 59).

BETTER HOMES AND GARDENS® BOOKS
Editorial Director: Don Dooley
Executive Editor: Gerald Knox
Art Director: Ernest Shelton
Assistant Art Director: Randall Yontz
Production and Copy Chief: David Kirchner
Food Editor: Doris Eby
Senior Associate Food Editor: Nancy Morton
Senior Food Editors: Sharyl Heiken,
    Elizabeth Strait
Associate Food Editors: Diane Nelson,
    Sandra Granseth, Flora Szatkowski
Graphic Designers: Sheryl Veenschoten
    Faith Berven, Harijs Priekulis

Better Homes and Gardens
TEST KITCHEN®

Our seal assures you that every recipe in *All-Time Favorite Beef Recipes* is endorsed by the Better Homes and Gardens Test Kitchen. Each recipe is tested for family appeal, practicality, and deliciousness.

Contents

USE BEEF CREATIVELY

Whether you're planning an elegant sit-down dinner or an informal backyard barbecue, beef is always at its versatile best. Preparation is as simple as roasting, broiling, frying, stewing, or even baking. Budget-wise, beef is available in a range from luxury roasts and steaks to economy ground beef. Knowing how to make the most of "best buy" cuts can be a challenge, regardless of your budget. These recipes are ready to help you do just that—again and again.

Put variety in your beef-centered menus. For the traditional roast, try *Golden Beef Pot Roast* and *Marinated Rare Roast Beef Platter.* Or serve steak in *Rainbow Beef,* short ribs in *Borsch-Style Stew,* or ground beef in *Tostada Pizza.* (See Index for recipe pages.)

1 Roasts to Remember

Although many cuts of beef share the name "roast," preparation methods usually depend on the tenderness of the cut to be roasted. More tender cuts can be dry-heat roasted, while less tender cuts need moist-heat or "pot roasting" to make them tender. Recipes for both of these methods—plus a quick-reference roasting chart—are included in this chapter.

Handsome *Boeuf En Croûte* is the perfect entrée for that special dinner. Marinated in wine, the beef roast is wrapped snugly in a flaky pastry lined with a fresh mushroom-liver pâté.

Roast Beef Supreme

Boeuf En Croûte

1 4-pound beef eye of the round
   roast
¾ cup Burgundy
¾ cup dry sherry
2 bay leaves
1 onion, quartered
½ pound fresh mushrooms,
   chopped (3 cups)
1 large leek, chopped (½ cup)
2 tablespoons butter *or*
   margarine
½ cup liver pâté *or* one 4¾-ounce
   can liver spread
¼ cup fine dry bread crumbs
2 cups all-purpose flour
½ teaspoon salt
⅔ cup shortening
⅓ to ½ cup cold water
1 beaten egg
¾ cup water
½ cup cold water
3 tablespoons all-purpose flour
   Salt
   Pepper

Place meat in clear plastic bag; set in deep bowl. Combine Burgundy, dry sherry, bay leaves, and onion. Pour over meat in bag; close. Chill overnight; turn bag occasionally to distribute the marinade.

Next day, remove meat from bag; reserve marinade. Place meat on rack in shallow roasting pan. Insert meat thermometer. Roast at 425° till thermometer registers 130°, about 55 minutes. Remove meat from pan; cool 20 minutes. Reserve drippings. Trim any fat from meat.

Meanwhile, cook mushrooms and leek in butter till tender, about 6 minutes. Remove from heat; stir in pâté, crumbs, and *3 tablespoons* of the reserved marinade. (Save remaining marinade.) Cover; chill at least 1 hour.

Stir together the 2 cups flour and ½ teaspoon salt. Cut in shortening till size of small peas. Gradually add ⅓ to ½ cup cold water, *1 tablespoon* at a time, tossing with fork till all is moistened. Form into a ball.

On floured surface roll dough to a 14x12-inch rectangle. Spread mushroom mixture to within 1 inch of edges. Center meat atop. Overlap long sides. Brush edges with egg; seal. Trim excess pastry from ends; fold up. Brush with egg; seal. Place roast, seam down, on greased baking sheet. Brush egg over all. Reroll pastry trimmings. Cut into strips; crisscross on roast. Brush with remaining egg.

Bake at 425° till pastry is golden, 30 to 35 minutes (meat will be rare). Heat ¾ cup water with reserved drippings till solids dissolve. Mix ½ cup cold water with 3 tablespoons flour; stir into drippings with ¼ *cup* reserved marinade. Cook and stir till bubbly; season with salt and pepper. Serve with roast. Makes 12 servings.

Beef Wellington

1 4-pound beef tenderloin
2 cups all-purpose flour
½ teaspoon salt
⅔ cup shortening
⅓ to ½ cup cold water
2 2¾-ounce cans liver pâté
1 beaten egg
1½ cups water
2 teaspoons instant beef
   bouillon granules
½ cup cold water
¼ cup all-purpose flour
⅓ cup Burgundy
½ teaspoon dried basil, crushed
   Salt
   Pepper
   Parsley sprigs

Place beef on rack in shallow roasting pan. Insert meat thermometer. Roast at 425° till thermometer registers 130°, about 45 minutes. Remove from pan; cool. Reserve drippings.

Stir 2 cups flour with ½ teaspoon salt; cut in shortening till size of small peas. Add ⅓ to ½ cup cold water, *1 tablespoon* at a time, tossing with fork till all is moistened. Form into ball. On floured surface roll to a 14x12-inch rectangle; spread with pâté to within ½ inch of edges.

Center meat atop. Overlap long sides. Brush on egg; seal. Trim excess pastry from ends; fold up. Brush on egg; seal. Place, seam down, on greased baking sheet. Reroll trimmings; make cutouts. Place on meat; brush remaining egg over pastry. Bake at 425° for 35 minutes (meat will be rare).

Heat and stir reserved drippings with 1½ cups water and bouillon granules till granules dissolve. Mix ½ cup cold water with ¼ cup flour; stir into hot mixture with Burgundy and basil. Cook and stir till bubbly; season with salt and pepper. Garnish with parsley; pass gravy. Serves 12.

Standing Rib Roast with Yorkshire Pudding

1 **4-pound beef rib roast,**
  large end
  Salt
  Pepper
4 **eggs**
2 **cups milk**
2 **cups all-purpose flour**
1 **teaspoon salt**

Place roast, fat side up, in 15½x10½x2-inch roasting pan. Season with salt and pepper. Insert meat thermometer. Roast, uncovered, at 325° till meat thermometer registers 140° for rare (about 2½ hours); 160° for medium (about 3 hours); and 170° for well done (about 3¼ hours). Remove from pan. Cover; keep warm. Reserve ¼ cup drippings.

Increase oven to 400°. In bowl beat eggs at low speed of electric mixer ½ minute. Add milk; beat 15 seconds. Add flour and salt; beat smooth, 2 minutes. Pour *half* the reserved drippings into *each* of two 9x9x2-inch baking pans. Divide batter between pans. Bake in 400° oven about 30 minutes. Cut into squares. Serve with roast. Serves 8.

Rump Roast with Vegetables

1 **4-pound boneless beef round**
  rump roast
¼ **teaspoon salt**
⅛ **teaspoon dried marjoram,**
  crushed
⅛ **teaspoon dried thyme,**
  crushed
  Dash pepper
8 **medium potatoes, peeled**
  and halved
8 **medium carrots, cut up**
¼ **cup all-purpose flour**
1 **tablespoon snipped parsley**
¾ **teaspoon salt**
  Dash pepper
  Dash dried marjoram, crushed
  Dash dried thyme, crushed

Place meat, fat side up, on rack in shallow roasting pan. Combine the ¼ teaspoon salt, the ⅛ teaspoon marjoram, the ⅛ teaspoon thyme, and the dash pepper; rub into meat. Roast, uncovered, at 325° till meat thermometer registers 150° to 170°, about 2¼ hours.

Meanwhile, in separate saucepans cook potatoes and carrots in boiling, salted water 15 minutes; drain. About 45 minutes before roast is done, place vegetables in drippings around roast, turning to coat. When done, transfer meat and vegetables to serving platter; keep warm. Sprinkle vegetables with additional snipped parsley, if desired.

Pour meat juices and fat into large measuring cup. Skim off fat, reserving 3 tablespoons. Add water to juices to make 2 cups; set aside. Return reserved fat to pan. Stir in flour; cook and stir over low heat till blended. Remove from heat. Add meat juices all at once; blend. Stir in snipped parsley, the ¾ teaspoon salt, dash pepper, dash marjoram, and dash thyme. Cook and stir till thickened and bubbly. Simmer 2 to 3 minutes more. Pass gravy with the roast. Serves 8 to 10.

Stuffed Rolled Rib Roast

4 **ounces thinly sliced, fully**
  cooked ham, chopped (1 cup)
3 **slices bacon, snipped**
¼ **cup chopped onion**
2 **tablespoons chopped pimiento-**
  stuffed green olives
1 **clove garlic, minced**
1 **beaten egg**
1 **4- to 5-pound boneless beef**
  rib roast

In bowl combine chopped ham, snipped bacon, onion, olives, garlic, and beaten egg. Unroll roast; spread ham mixture over meat. Reroll roast; tie securely.

Place roast, fat side up, on rack in shallow roasting pan. Roast, uncovered, at 325° about 3 hours for rare. Let stand about 15 minutes. Remove strings and carve. Makes 12 to 14 servings.

Re-create a dinner in the style of merrie olde England with a menu featuring *Standing Rib Roast with Yorkshire Pudding.* Buttered Brussels sprouts are a popular accompaniment.

Teriyaki Roast Beef

1 cup soy sauce
½ cup cooking oil
¼ cup light molasses
1 tablespoon ground ginger
1 tablespoon dry mustard
8 cloves garlic, minced
1 6- to 7-pound boneless
   beef rib roast

In a deep bowl or crock combine the soy sauce, cooking oil, molasses, ground ginger, dry mustard, and minced garlic. Add meat to marinade mixture, turning to coat. Cover and refrigerate overnight, spooning the marinade over meat occasionally.

Remove roast from bowl, reserving marinade. Place roast, fat side up, on rack in shallow roasting pan. Insert meat thermometer. Roast at 325° till meat thermometer registers 140° for rare (about 3 hours); 160° for medium (about 4 hours); or 170° for well done (about 4¾ hours). While the meat is roasting, baste several times with the reserved marinade. Remove roast from oven; cover with foil. Let stand about 15 minutes; remove strings and carve thinly across the grain. Makes about 14 servings.

Barbecued Rump Roast

2½ cups vinegar
2½ cups water
 2 medium onions, sliced
 1 medium lemon, sliced
12 whole cloves
 6 whole black peppercorns
 2 or 3 bay leaves
 1 tablespoon salt
 1 3-pound boneless beef round
    rump roast

In deep bowl combine vinegar, water, onions, lemon, cloves, peppercorns, bay leaves, and salt. Add meat to marinade mixture, turning to coat. Cover; refrigerate 2 to 3 days, turning meat occasionally. Drain meat; reserving marinade. Center roast on spit. Adjust holding forks; test balance. Insert meat thermometer near center of roast but not touching metal rod. Attach spit. Place drip pan under meat. Turn on motor. Roast over *slow* coals till thermometer registers 160° for medium, about 1½ hours. Baste meat occasionally with reserved marinade during the last 30 minutes. Let stand 15 minutes before carving. Makes 8 servings.

Roast Sirloin with Zippy Mustard Sauce

2 beaten egg yolks
2 tablespoons prepared mustard
2 tablespoons vinegar
1 tablespoon water
1 tablespoon prepared
   horseradish
1 tablespoon butter *or*
   margarine
1 tablespoon sugar
½ teaspoon salt
½ cup whipping cream
1 6-pound boneless beef sirloin
   roast
   Garlic salt
   Pepper

In small saucepan combine egg yolks, prepared mustard, vinegar, water, prepared horseradish, butter, sugar, and salt; mix well. Cook and stir over very low heat till sauce is thickened, about 2 minutes. Remove from heat. Stir till sauce is smooth; cool. Whip cream; fold into mustard mixture and chill.

Place roast, fat side up, on rack in shallow roasting pan. Sprinkle generously with garlic salt and pepper. Insert meat thermometer. Roast at 350° till meat thermometer registers 140° for rare, 1½ to 1¾ hours. Let roast stand about 15 minutes before carving. Serve with mustard sauce. Makes 14 to 16 servings.

Italian-Style Popovers (see page 13) are a light and tender addition to any roast. This easy-to-make variation of the traditional is seasoned with Italian salad dressing mix.

Potpourri Sauced Tenderloin

½ cup finely chopped onion
½ cup catsup
2 tablespoons vinegar
2 tablespoons cooking oil
1 tablespoon snipped parsley
2 teaspoons sugar
2 teaspoons Worcestershire sauce
1 teaspoon dried thyme, crushed
1 teaspoon prepared horseradish
1 teaspoon salt
¼ teaspoon chili powder
1 clove garlic, minced
1 cup water
1 2-pound beef tenderloin
  Salt
  Pepper

In 1-quart saucepan combine onion, catsup, vinegar, oil, parsley, sugar, Worcestershire, thyme, horseradish, 1 teaspoon salt, chili powder, and garlic. Blend in water.

Bring mixture to boiling; reduce heat. Boil, uncovered, over medium-low heat till sauce is of medium-thick consistency, 20 to 25 minutes.

Meanwhile, place meat on rack in shallow roasting pan; sprinkle with a little salt and pepper. Insert meat thermometer. Roast at 425° for 30 minutes. Remove from oven; brush with some of the sauce. Return to oven and roast till thermometer registers 140°, about 15 minutes more; brush occasionally with sauce. Let stand 15 minutes before carving. Serve remaining sauce with meat. Makes 8 servings.

Quick and Easy Marinated Beef Tenderloin

1 2-pound beef tenderloin
½ cup catsup
½ cup water
1 envelope Italian salad
    dressing mix
1 teaspoon prepared mustard
¼ teaspoon Worcestershire sauce

Pierce meat on all sides with a long-tined fork; place in plastic bag set in deep bowl. Combine catsup, water, dry salad dressing mix, mustard, and Worcestershire; pour over meat in bag and close. Refrigerate 24 hours; occasionally press bag against meat to distribute marinade evenly.

Remove meat from bag, reserving marinade. Place meat on rack in shallow roasting pan. Insert meat thermometer. Roast at 425° till thermometer registers 140° for rare, 45 to 50 minutes; baste occasionally with *half* of the reserved marinade. Let stand 15 minutes before carving.

In saucepan, heat remaining marinade to boiling; spoon over meat. Makes 6 to 8 servings.

Cold Filet of Beef Waldorf

1 2-pound beef tenderloin
2 large carrots
½ teaspoon salt
⅛ teaspoon pepper
6 tablespoons liver pâté *or*
    liver spread
2 cups water
2 envelopes unflavored gelatin
2 teaspoons instant beef
    bouillon granules
1½ cups rosé wine

With a sharp knife cut a deep slit horizontally in meat. Cut off narrow ends of carrots. (Carrots should be equal to each other in diameter and, when placed end to end, as long as the roast.) Insert whole carrots into pocket of roast.

Rub meat with salt and pepper; place on rack in shallow roasting pan. Insert meat thermometer. Roast at 425° till thermometer registers 140°, about 50 minutes. Cool 30 minutes. Remove carrots and discard; stuff the pocket with liver pâté or liver spread. Cover and chill meat.

In saucepan combine water, gelatin, and beef bouillon granules; stir to dissolve over low heat. Stir in wine; chill till mixture is slightly thickened.

Transfer chilled meat to a shallow pan. Carefully spoon about ½ cup of the gelatin mixture over meat; chill meat till gelatin coating is nearly set. Keep remaining gelatin mixture at room temperature.

Repeat spooning gelatin mixture over meat and chilling 3 times. Cover loosely; chill 5 hours or overnight.

To serve, cut roast into ½-inch slices; arrange on serving platter. Dice excess gelatin from bottom of pan; arrange around meat as garnish. Makes 10 to 12 servings.

Marinated Rare Roast Beef Platter (pictured on page 4)

1 3-pound boneless beef round
    rump roast
2 10-ounce packages frozen
    asparagus spears
1 4½-ounce jar sliced mushrooms,
    drained
1 cup cooking oil
½ cup vinegar
2 small cloves garlic, minced
2 teaspoons sugar
1½ teaspoons salt
1½ teaspoons dry mustard
    Dash pepper
12 cherry tomatoes

Place meat, fat side up, on rack in shallow roasting pan. Insert meat thermometer. Roast at 325° till thermometer registers 145°, for 1½ to 2 hours. Cool slightly; slice meat.

Cook asparagus spears according to package directions; drain. In shallow baking dish arrange sliced meat, asparagus spears, and sliced mushrooms.

In screw-top jar combine cooking oil, vinegar, garlic, sugar, salt, dry mustard, and pepper; shake well. Pour marinade mixture over meat and vegetables in dish. Cover and refrigerate for 2 to 3 hours.

To serve, drain meat and vegetables. Arrange meat and asparagus spears on large platter. Spoon mushrooms over meat; garnish with cherry tomatoes. Makes 8 servings.

Preparing Beef Roasts

Cut	Approximate Weight (Pounds)	Internal Temperature on Removal from Oven	Approximate Cooking Time (Total Time)
Roast meat at constant oven temperature of 325° unless otherwise indicated.			
Rib Roast	4 to 6	140° (rare) 160° (medium) 170° (well done)	2¼ to 2¾ hrs. 2¾ to 3¼ hrs. 3¼ to 3½ hrs.
Rib Roast	6 to 8	140° (rare) 160° (medium) 170° (well done)	2½ to 3 hrs. 3 to 3½ hrs. 3¾ to 4 hrs.
Boneless Rib Roast	5 to 7	140° (rare) 160° (medium) 170° (well done)	3¼ to 3½ hrs. 3¾ to 4 hrs. 4½ to 4¾ hrs.
Boneless Round Rump Roast	4 to 6	150° to 170°	2 to 2½ hrs.
Round Tip Roast	3½ to 4	140° to 170°	2 to 2¾ hrs.
Rib Eye Roast (Roast at 350°)	4 to 6	140° (rare) 160° (medium) 170° (well done)	1½ to 1¾ hrs. 1¾ hrs. 2 hrs.
Tenderloin Roast (Roast at 425°)	4 to 6	140° (rare)	45 min. to 1 hr.

Season the roast by sprinkling with a little salt and pepper. Insert a meat thermometer in center of the roast so that bulb reaches the thickest part of the lean meat. Make sure the bulb does not rest in fat or touch bone. Place roast, fat side up, on rack in a shallow roasting pan. Do not cover, add water, or baste. Except as noted above, roast at 325° till the thermometer registers desired internal temperature. To check, push thermometer into meat a little farther. If temperature drops, continue cooking the roast to desired temperature. Let meat stand 15 minutes for easier carving. (Remove string from rolled and tied roasts.) Carve meat across the grain.

Italian-Style Popovers (pictured on page 11)

2 eggs
½ cup milk
½ cup water
1 cup all-purpose flour
1 tablespoon Italian salad dressing mix
¼ teaspoon salt
1 tablespoon cooking oil

In small mixing bowl combine eggs, milk, water, flour, dry Italian salad dressing mix, and salt. Beat at medium speed of electric mixer or with rotary beater 1½ minutes. Add cooking oil; beat ½ minute longer.

Pour batter into 6 greased 6-ounce custard cups. Bake at 475° for 15 minutes; reduce oven temperature to 350°. Bake popovers 25 minutes longer. Makes 6 servings.

Pot Roast Variations

Sauerbraten

2½ cups water
1½ cups red wine vinegar
1 tablespoon sugar
1 tablespoon salt
¼ teaspoon ground ginger
12 whole cloves
6 bay leaves
6 whole black peppercorns
2 medium onions, sliced
1 lemon, sliced
1 4-pound boneless beef round
   rump roast
2 tablespoons cooking oil
½ cup chopped onion
½ cup chopped carrot
¼ cup chopped celery
1 cup broken gingersnaps
⅔ cup water
   Hot buttered noodles

In crock or large bowl combine the 2½ cups water, wine vinegar, sugar, salt, ginger, cloves, bay leaves, peppercorns, sliced onion and lemon; add meat. Cover; refrigerate 36 to 72 hours, turning meat occasionally. Remove meat; wipe dry with paper toweling. Strain marinade; reserve.

In Dutch oven brown roast on all sides in hot oil. Add reserved marinade, chopped onion, carrot, and celery. Cover; simmer till meat is tender, about 2 hours.

Transfer meat to platter; keep hot. Reserve 2 cups of the liquid in Dutch oven; stir in gingersnaps and the ⅔ cup water. Cook and stir till thickened and bubbly. Serve meat and gravy with noodles. Makes 8 to 10 servings.

Rump Roast Supreme

1 4- to 6-pound boneless beef
   round rump roast
2 tablespoons shortening
1 cup dry red wine
1 cup beef broth
½ cup chopped onion
1 teaspoon salt
¼ teaspoon ground thyme
¼ teaspoon pepper
1 bay leaf
1 clove garlic, minced
¼ cup all-purpose flour

In Dutch oven brown meat slowly on all sides in hot shortening. Add ½ *cup* of the dry red wine, the beef broth, onion, salt, thyme, pepper, bay leaf, and garlic. Cover; roast at 325° till meat is tender, 2½ to 3 hours.

Remove strings from roast. Transfer meat to serving platter; keep warm. Discard bay leaf. Skim excess fat from pan juices; add water to juices to make 2 cups.

Return juices to pan. Blend remaining ½ cup wine with flour; stir into juices. Cook and stir till thickened and bubbly. Pass gravy with meat. Makes 8 to 10 servings.

Pot Roast Dip Sandwiches

1 3-pound beef round rump roast
¼ cup all-purpose flour
2 tablespoons shortening
   Salt
   Pepper
½ cup water
2 10½-ounce cans condensed
   beef broth
2 teaspoons instant minced
   onion
1 teaspoon Worcestershire sauce
12 hard rolls

Coat meat with flour. In Dutch oven brown meat on all sides in hot shortening. Season with salt and pepper. Remove from heat; add ½ cup water. Cover; return to heat. Simmer till tender, 2 to 2½ hours. Add water, if needed.

Pour off pan juices into measuring cup; skim off fat. Add water to juices, if needed, to make 2 cups. In saucepan combine pan juices, beef broth, onion, and Worcestershire. Bring to boiling; reduce heat. Simmer 5 minutes.

Slice roast as thinly as possible. Split hard rolls lengthwise, cutting almost all the way through. Place a few slices of meat in each roll. Serve each sandwich with about ⅓ *cup* of the hot broth. Makes 12 servings.

Bold and spicy *Sauerbraten* is draped with gingersnap gravy atop a bed of noodles. This German specialty is characterized by chilling the roast for 2 to 3 days in a sweet-sour marinade.

Saucy Pot Roast

  1 2½-pound beef chuck pot roast
  2 cups tomato juice
  ¼ cup red wine vinegar
  2 teaspoons Worcestershire
     sauce
1½ teaspoons salt
  1 teaspoon sugar
  ½ teaspoon dried basil, crushed
  ½ teaspoon dried thyme, crushed
  ¼ teaspoon pepper
  1 clove garlic, minced
12 small potatoes, peeled
  6 small onions
  6 carrots, halved crosswise
  ½ cup cold water
  3 tablespoons all-purpose flour

Trim excess fat from meat. Place meat in clear plastic bag; set in deep bowl. Mix tomato juice, vinegar, Worcestershire, salt, sugar, basil, thyme, pepper, and garlic. Pour over meat; close bag. Marinate overnight in refrigerator; turn bag occasionally to distribute marinade.

Next day, transfer roast and marinade from bag to Dutch oven. Cover; simmer 1 hour. Add potatoes, onions, and carrots. Cover and simmer till meat and vegetables are tender, 45 to 60 minutes longer.

Transfer meat and vegetables to serving platter; keep warm. Pour pan juices into measuring cup; skim off fat. Measure 2 cups juices; return to pan. Blend cold water and flour; stir into pan juices. Cook and stir till thickened and bubbly. Serve with meat and vegetables. Serves 6.

Polynesian Pot Roast

    1 3-pound beef chuck pot roast
    ¼ cup all-purpose flour
    2 tablespoons shortening
    1 8-ounce can pineapple slices
        (juice pack)
    ¼ cup soy sauce
    3 tablespoons lemon juice
    2 tablespoons brown sugar
    ½ teaspoon dried basil, crushed
    1 clove garlic, minced
    ¼ cup cold water
    2 tablespoons cornstarch

Trim excess fat from meat. Coat meat with flour. In Dutch oven brown meat on all sides in hot shortening. Drain pineapple, reserving juice. Mix reserved juice, soy, lemon juice, brown sugar, basil, and garlic. Pour over roast in Dutch oven. Cover; roast at 350° till meat is tender, about 2 hours. Baste occasionally with soy mixture, if desired. During last 10 minutes of cooking, top roast with pineapple.

Transfer roast and pineapple to serving platter; keep warm. Pour pan juices into measuring cup; skim off fat. Add water to juices to make 2 cups; return to pan. Blend cold water and cornstarch; stir into pan juices. Cook and stir till thickened and bubbly. Drizzle roast with a little of the sauce; pass remaining sauce. Makes 6 servings.

Fruited Pot Roast

    1 3-pound beef chuck pot roast
    2 tablespoons shortening
 1½ teaspoons salt
    ¼ teaspoon pepper
    ½ cup Burgundy
    ½ cup finely chopped onion
    ⅓ cup finely chopped carrot
    1 clove garlic, minced
    1 11-ounce package mixed dried
        fruits (1¾ cups)
 1½ cups hot water
    ⅓ cup cold water
    3 tablespoons all-purpose flour
        Salt
        Pepper

Trim excess fat from meat. In Dutch oven brown meat on all sides in hot shortening. Sprinkle with 1½ teaspoons salt and ¼ teaspoon pepper; add Burgundy, onion, carrot, and garlic. Cover tightly; simmer 1½ hours.

Meanwhile, cut up large pieces of dried fruit. Pour 1½ cups hot water over fruit; let stand 1 hour. Drain fruit, reserving liquid. Place fruit atop meat. Cover; cook till meat is tender, about 45 minutes more.

Remove meat and fruit to serving platter; keep warm. Pour pan juices into measuring cup; skim off fat. Add reserved fruit liquid to pan juices to make 1½ cups; return to pan. Blend cold water and flour; stir into pan juices. Cook and stir till thickened and bubbly. Season to taste with salt and pepper. Serve with roast. Makes 6 to 8 servings.

Spicy Beef with Parsley Dumplings

    1 3- to 4-pound beef chuck pot
        roast
    2 tablespoons shortening
    1 16-ounce can tomatoes, cut up
    ¼ cup red wine vinegar
    1 teaspoon salt
    1 teaspoon sugar
    ½ teaspoon mixed pickling spice
    ¼ teaspoon pepper
    1 clove garlic, minced
    1 cup all-purpose flour
    2 tablespoons snipped parsley
    2 teaspoons baking powder
    ½ teaspoon salt
    1 egg
    ¼ cup milk
    2 tablespoons butter, melted
    2 tablespoons cornstarch

Trim excess fat from meat. In Dutch oven or large skillet brown meat slowly on all sides in hot shortening. Add undrained tomatoes, wine vinegar, 1 teaspoon salt, sugar, pickling spice, pepper, garlic, and ¼ cup water. Cover and simmer till meat is tender, 2 to 2½ hours. When meat is almost tender, prepare dumplings.

Stir together flour, parsley, baking powder, and ½ teaspoon salt. Combine egg, milk, and melted butter; add to flour mixture, stirring just till blended. Drop dough by tablespoonfuls directly onto meat in boiling broth. Return to boiling, then reduce heat and cover tightly. Simmer till dumplings are done, 12 to 15 minutes; *do not lift cover.*

Transfer dumplings and roast to serving platter; keep warm. Pour pan juices into measuring cup; skim off fat. Add water to juices, if needed, to make 2 cups; return to pan.

Blend ¼ cup cold water with cornstarch; stir into juices. Cook and stir till thickened and bubbly. Season to taste with salt and pepper. Cook and stir 2 to 3 minutes more. Serve with roast and dumplings. Makes 6 to 8 servings.

Golden Beef Pot Roast (pictured on page 4)

1   3- to 3½-pound beef chuck
      pot roast
3   tablespoons all-purpose flour
1   teaspoon salt
¼   teaspoon pepper
2   tablespoons cooking oil
¼   cup water
¼   teaspoon celery seed
¼   teaspoon dried oregano,
      crushed
½   cup water
¼   cup frozen orange juice
      concentrate, thawed
1½ pounds sweet potatoes,
      peeled and halved
      (4 medium potatoes)
2   medium onions, quartered
¼   cup cold water
2   tablespoons all-purpose flour
    Salt
    Pepper
    Parsley sprigs

Trim excess fat from meat. Combine 3 tablespoons flour, 1 teaspoon salt, and ¼ teaspoon pepper; coat meat with flour mixture. In Dutch oven brown meat slowly on all sides in hot oil; drain off excess fat. Add ¼ cup water, celery seed, and oregano. Cover tightly; simmer 1½ hours.

Combine ½ cup water and orange juice concentrate; pour over meat. Add potatoes and onions, pushing vegetables down into liquid. Cover; simmer till meat and vegetables are tender, about 1 hour longer.

Transfer meat and vegetables to platter; keep warm. Pour pan juices into measuring cup; skim off fat. Add enough water to juices to equal 1¼ cups. Blend ¼ cup cold water with 2 tablespoons flour; stir into juices. Cook and stir till thickened and bubbly. Season with salt and pepper.

To serve, spoon a little gravy over meat and vegetables. Garnish platter with parsley sprigs, if desired. Pass remaining gravy. Makes 6 to 8 servings.

Beef and Bean Pot Roast

1   3-pound beef chuck pot roast
2   tablespoons cooking oil
2   cups water
1   cup chopped onion
1   cup dry lima beans, rinsed
½   cup catsup
1   teaspoon salt
⅛   teaspoon pepper
1   clove garlic, minced
2   teaspoons mixed pickling spice
3   carrots, sliced (about 1½
      cups)

Trim excess fat from meat. In Dutch oven brown meat on all sides in hot oil; remove meat. Drain off fat. In same Dutch oven combine water, chopped onion, dry lima beans, catsup, salt, pepper, and garlic.

Tie mixed pickling spice in cheesecloth bag; add to bean mixture in Dutch oven. Place meat atop beans. Simmer, covered, till meat and beans are almost tender, about 2 hours. Add additional water during cooking, if necessary, to keep beans covered. Add sliced carrots; simmer, covered, 30 minutes more. Discard spice bag. Makes 6 to 8 servings.

Pot Roast Tips

It's easy to make a perfect pot roast when you understand the method. The term "pot roasting" refers to cooking a piece of meat in a covered pan. Since liquid is usually added, braising is another term sometimes used.

The first step is to trim away any excess fat. For a rich brown color, coat the roast on all sides with all-purpose flour. Slowly brown the roast in hot fat using shortening, cooking oil, or drippings from the melted fat trimmings. Add the desired liquid (usually beef broth, tomato juice, or water) and the seasonings. Cover and cook over low heat in a Dutch oven atop the range, *or* in a 325° oven, *or* in an electric skillet set at about 220°.

Sour Creamed Pot Roast

2 slices bacon
1 3- to 4-pound beef chuck pot
   roast
¾ cup chopped onion
¾ cup water
1 teaspoon salt
¼ teaspoon ground cumin
⅛ teaspoon pepper
1 bay leaf
½ cup dairy sour cream
2 tablespoons all-purpose flour
2 tablespoons snipped parsley
½ teaspoon Kitchen Bouquet
   (optional)
   Hot cooked noodles

Cook bacon till crisp. Drain; reserve drippings. Crumble bacon. Trim excess fat from meat. In Dutch oven brown meat on all sides in drippings. Add onion, water, salt, cumin, pepper, and bay leaf. Cover; roast at 325° for 1½ to 2 hours.

Remove meat to platter; keep warm. Skim fat from pan juices; discard bay leaf. Blend sour cream with flour. Stir about ¼ cup of the pan juices into sour cream mixture; return to pan. Cook and stir till thickened; *do not boil.* Stir in parsley, bacon, and Kitchen Bouquet. Season with salt and pepper. Serve with roast and noodles. Serves 6 to 8.

Crockery cooker directions: Prepare bacon as above; reserve drippings. Trim excess fat from roast; cut in half to fit in electric slow crockery cooker. Brown meat on all sides in drippings; transfer to cooker. Combine onion, *only ¼ cup* water, salt, cumin, pepper, and bay leaf; pour over meat. Cover; cook on low-heat setting 8 to 10 hours.

Remove roast; discard bay leaf. Skim fat from cooking juices; pour juices into saucepan. Return roast to cooker; cover. Blend sour cream with *3 tablespoons* flour. Stir about ¼ cup of juices into sour cream mixture; return to pan. Cook and stir till thickened; *do not boil.* Stir in parsley, bacon, and Kitchen Bouquet. Season and serve as above.

Savory Blade Pot Roast

1 3-pound beef blade pot roast
1 tablespoon cooking oil
¼ cup red wine vinegar
¼ cup catsup
2 tablespoons soy sauce
2 tablespoons Worcestershire
   sauce
1 teaspoon dried rosemary,
   crushed
½ teaspoon garlic powder
½ teaspoon dry mustard

Trim excess fat from roast. In Dutch oven brown meat slowly on both sides in hot oil; remove from heat. Drain off fat; sprinkle roast with a little salt.

Combine wine vinegar, catsup, soy sauce, Worcestershire, rosemary, garlic powder, dry mustard, and ¼ cup water; pour mixture over roast. Return to heat. Cover tightly; simmer till meat is tender, 1½ to 1¾ hours.

Transfer meat to serving platter. Skim excess fat from pan juices; spoon juices over meat. Makes 6 to 8 servings.

Easy Pot Roast Dinner

1 envelope instant meat marinade
⅔ cup vegetable juice cocktail
1 3- to 4-pound beef chuck pot
   roast
2 15- or 16-ounce cans whole
   white potatoes
1 16-ounce can cut green beans
1 3-ounce can sliced mushrooms
½ cup cold water
2 tablespoons all-purpose flour

In Dutch oven mix marinade and vegetable juice. Trim excess fat from meat; place meat in marinade mixture. Marinate 15 minutes, piercing meat with long-tined fork and turning often. Cover; simmer till nearly tender, about 2¼ hours.

Drain potatoes, beans, and mushrooms; add to Dutch oven. Simmer 15 minutes more. Transfer roast and vegetables to platter; keep warm. Skim fat from pan juices. Blend cold water with flour; stir into pan juices. Cook and stir till thickened and bubbly. Spoon some of the gravy over roast; pass remaining gravy. Makes 6 to 8 servings.

Vegetable-sauced *Swedish Pot Roast* features cloves and anchovies as the special seasonings. Prepared with chuck pot roast, this dish rates high as a cost-cutting entrée.

Swedish Pot Roast

1 3- to 4-pound beef chuck pot roast
1 teaspoon salt
4 whole cloves
2 medium onions, quartered
1 cup chopped carrots
½ cup chopped celery
⅓ cup water
1 tablespoon corn syrup
3 anchovy fillets
¼ cup cold water
2 tablespoons all-purpose flour
  Salt
  Pepper

Trim excess fat from meat. Sprinkle 1 teaspoon salt in Dutch oven; brown meat slowly on all sides in Dutch oven. Stick cloves into onions. Add to meat along with carrots, celery, the ⅓ cup water, corn syrup, and anchovies. Cover and simmer till meat is tender, about 2½ hours.

Transfer meat to serving platter; keep warm. Skim fat from pan juices. Blend the ¼ cup cold water with flour; stir into juices. (Mash carrot if desired.) Cook and stir till thickened and bubbly. Season to taste with salt and pepper; pass with roast. Makes 6 to 8 servings.

Unconventional preparation is a plus for *Peach-Glazed Corned Beef*. Instead of simmering atop the range, the brisket is baked in a covered pan with added water. Preserves make the glaze.

Peach-Glazed Corned Beef

1 3-pound corned beef brisket
  (*or* 1 3- to 4-pound corned
  beef for oven roasting)
2 cups water
4 small apples
½ cup water
⅓ cup peach preserves
¼ teaspoon ground ginger

Rinse brisket in cold water to remove pickling juices. Place, fat side up, on rack in shallow roasting pan. Add 2 cups water; cover with foil. Roast at 325° for 2 hours. Uncover; drain cooking liquid and discard. (Or prepare corned beef for oven roasting by package directions.)

Cut apples in half lengthwise and core. Arrange apple halves, skin side up, around corned beef in roasting pan; add ½ cup water to pan. Return to oven; continue roasting, uncovered, 30 minutes longer.

Combine peach preserves and ground ginger. Turn apple halves, skin side down. Spoon peach glaze over apple halves and corned beef; return to oven and cook till glaze is hot, about 15 minutes longer. Makes 6 to 8 servings.

New England Boiled Dinner

1 3- to 4-pound corned beef
  brisket
  Water
4 ounces salt pork (optional)
6 small onions
4 medium potatoes, peeled and
  quartered
4 medium carrots, quartered
3 medium parsnips, peeled and
  cut in chunks
2 medium rutabagas, peeled and
  cubed
1 small cabbage, cored and cut
  in wedges
  Salt
  Pepper

Place corned beef in large kettle or Dutch oven; add water to cover meat. Add salt pork, if desired. Bring to boiling; reduce heat and simmer, covered, till corned beef is tender, about 2½ hours.

Remove corned beef and salt pork from kettle. Add onions, potatoes, carrots, parsnips, and rutabagas to cooking liquid. Cover; cook 15 minutes. Add cabbage; cover and cook till cabbage is tender, 15 to 20 minutes more.

Return corned beef to kettle; heat through. Transfer corned beef and vegetables to serving platter. Season to taste with salt and pepper. Makes 6 to 8 servings.

Brisket of Beef with Horseradish Sauce

1 3- to 4-pound fresh beef
  brisket
2 cups water
½ cup chopped onion
2 cloves garlic, minced
2 bay leaves
3 tablespoons grated fresh
  horseradish
2 tablespoons vinegar
1 tablespoon prepared mustard
½ teaspoon salt
  Dash cayenne
  Dash paprika
½ cup whipping cream

Trim excess fat from meat; place meat in 4-quart Dutch oven. Add water, onion, garlic, and bay leaves. Cover; simmer till meat is tender, 2½ to 3 hours. Drain meat; slice.

Meanwhile, in bowl combine horseradish, vinegar, mustard, salt, cayenne, and paprika. Whip cream till soft peaks form; fold in horseradish mixture. Serve sauce with sliced beef brisket. Makes 6 servings.

Fresh Brisket with Kraut

1 2-pound fresh beef brisket
2 medium onions, sliced
½ cup water
1 teaspoon salt
1 bay leaf
1 27-ounce can sauerkraut
1 medium potato, peeled and
   shredded (1 cup)
1 teaspoon caraway seed

Trim excess fat from meat. Place meat, fat side down, in skillet; brown on both sides. Add onions, water, salt, and bay leaf. Cover and simmer 1½ hours.

Drain sauerkraut (rinse, if milder flavor is desired); add to meat with potato and caraway. Simmer, covered, till meat is tender, about 30 minutes longer. Remove the bay leaf. Makes 6 to 8 servings.

Cranberry Pot Roast

1 3- to 4-pound beef chuck
   pot roast
2 tablespoons all-purpose flour
1 teaspoon salt
1 teaspoon onion salt
¼ teaspoon pepper
2 tablespoons shortening
4 whole cloves
2 inches stick cinnamon
1 16-ounce can whole cranberry
   sauce
1 tablespoon vinegar

Trim excess fat from roast. Combine the flour, salt, onion salt, and pepper; rub into pot roast, using all of the flour mixture. In a Dutch oven, slowly brown the meat on all sides in hot shortening. Remove from heat; add cloves, cinnamon, and ½ cup water. Cover tightly; simmer till meat is tender, about 2½ hours. Add more water if necessary.

Spoon off the excess fat. Mix cranberry sauce, vinegar, and 2 tablespoons water; pour over meat. Cover and cook 10 to 15 minutes. Remove cloves and cinnamon; discard.

Transfer meat to serving platter. Skim excess fat from pan juices and pass juices with meat. Makes 6 to 8 servings.

Oven-Braised Brisket

1 3½- to 4-pound fresh beef
   brisket
1 cup chopped onion
½ cup sliced celery
½ cup sliced carrot
½ cup chopped green pepper
¼ cup water
2 whole cloves
2 whole allspice
1 clove garlic, halved
1 bay leaf
¼ teaspoon paprika
   Salt
   Pepper
½ cup all-purpose flour
1 14-ounce can beef broth
   (1¾ cups)

Trim excess fat from fresh beef brisket, reserving some of the trimmings. In large skillet heat reserved trimmings till about 2 tablespoons fat accumulate; discard trimmings. Brown meat on both sides in hot fat.

Transfer meat to a 12x7½x2-inch baking dish. Add onion, celery, carrot, green pepper, water, cloves, allspice, garlic (speared onto wooden pick), bay leaf, and paprika. Sprinkle with salt and pepper. Cover tightly with foil. Bake at 325° till meat is tender, about 3 hours.

Meanwhile, in medium saucepan heat flour over medium-high heat, stirring constantly, till flour turns a dark beige color, 10 to 15 minutes. Cool; reserve for gravy.

Transfer meat to serving platter. Remove cloves, allspice, garlic, and bay leaf. Drain vegetables, reserving cooking juices. Spoon vegetables over meat; keep warm.

In saucepan blend ¾ *cup* of the beef broth with browned flour. Pour reserved cooking juices into measuring cup; add remaining beef broth, plus water if necessary, to make 1½ cups liquid. Stir into flour mixture. Cook and stir till thickened and bubbly; cook and stir 2 minutes more. Serve gravy with meat and vegetables. Makes 6 to 8 servings.

Round Tip Roast with Italian Tomato Sauce

½ cup dry red wine
1 envelope instant meat
   marinade
1 4-pound beef round tip roast
½ of a 15½-ounce can marinara
   sauce (1 cup)
1 teaspoon sugar
1 medium onion, sliced
1 cup chopped celery
1 cup sliced fresh mushrooms
½ cup dairy sour cream
¼ cup cold water
¼ cup all-purpose flour
   Hot cooked spaghetti
   (optional)

Combine wine and dry marinade; marinate roast according to package directions. Drain roast, reserving marinade.

In Dutch oven combine reserved marinade, marinara sauce, and sugar; add roast. Cover and simmer for 1½ hours. Add onion, celery, and mushrooms; simmer, covered, till meat is tender, about 1 hour longer.

Transfer roast and vegetables to serving platter; keep warm. Pour pan juices into measuring cup; skim off fat. Return 2 cups of the pan juices to Dutch oven.

Combine sour cream and water; blend with flour. Stir flour mixture into pan juices in Dutch oven. Cook and stir till thickened and bubbly; pass with meat. Serve with hot cooked spaghetti, if desired. Makes 8 servings.

Vegetable-Stuffed Roast

¼ cup chopped celery
¼ cup chopped onion
¼ cup chopped carrot
2 tablespoons butter or
   margarine
1 teaspoon salt
1 teaspoon dried savory,
   crushed
½ teaspoon dried basil, crushed
¼ teaspoon dried thyme, crushed
⅛ teaspoon pepper
1 3- to 4-pound beef round tip
   roast
¾ cup dry red wine
½ cup water
½ cup cold water
⅓ cup all-purpose flour
½ teaspoon Kitchen Bouquet

In small skillet cook celery, onion, and carrot in butter till tender but not brown; cool slightly.

Combine salt, savory, basil, thyme, and pepper. Cut a horizontal slit in meaty end of roast. Rub herb mixture on all surfaces of meat, including pocket. Stuff pocket with cooked vegetable mixture; skewer closed.

Place roast, fat side up, on rack in shallow roasting pan. Combine wine and ½ cup water; pour over meat. Cover with foil; roast at 350° till meat is tender, 2 to 2½ hours.

Transfer meat to serving platter; keep warm. Pour pan juices into measuring cup; skim off fat. Add enough water to pan juices to equal 2½ cups liquid; pour into saucepan. Blend ½ cup cold water with flour and Kitchen Bouquet; stir into pan juices. Cook and stir till thickened and bubbly. Pass gravy with meat. Makes 10 to 12 servings.

Crumb-Topped Tomatoes (pictured on cover)

6 small tomatoes
¼ cup sliced green onion
   with tops
1 tablespoon butter or
   margarine
¼ cup fine dry bread crumbs
½ teaspoon dried dillweed
¼ teaspoon salt
   Dash Worcestershire sauce

Cut a thin slice from top of each tomato; sprinkle with a little salt and pepper. In small saucepan cook green onion in butter till tender but not brown; stir in crumbs, dillweed, salt, and Worcestershire sauce.

Sprinkle about 1 tablespoon of the crumb mixture atop each tomato. Place tomatoes in an 8x8x2-inch baking pan. Bake at 325° till heated through, about 25 minutes. Use as garnish with roasts.

2 Steaks for All Occasions

Make the most of the steaks in your menu with the helps in this chapter. When sirloin and other tender cuts are affordable, use the next five pages for ideas on how to serve them in the style they deserve. But when a trimmed budget calls for round steak or other less tender cuts, see the last part of the chapter for specific recipes to help make these cuts deliciously tender.

When it comes to elegant dining, *Filet of Beef à la Bearnaise* meets the challenge deliciously. A classic tarragon-flavored bearnaise sauce enhances the tenderloin steaks.

Steaks that Cost More

Filet of Beef à la Bearnaise

6 beef tenderloin steaks, cut
    ¾ inch thick
Salt
Pepper
3 tablespoons tarragon vinegar
1 teaspoon finely chopped
    shallots *or* green onion
    with tops
¼ teaspoon freshly ground black
    pepper
1 tablespoon cold water
4 egg yolks
½ cup butter, softened
¼ teaspoon dried tarragon,
    crushed

Place steaks on cold rack of broiler pan. Broil 3 inches from heat to desired doneness, turning steaks once. Allow 10 to 12 minutes total broiling time for medium. Season steaks with a little salt and pepper.

Meanwhile, in saucepan combine tarragon vinegar, chopped shallots or green onion, and freshly ground black pepper; simmer for 2 minutes. Add cold water.

Beat egg yolks in top of double boiler (not over water). Slowly blend in vinegar mixture. Stir a few tablespoons of the butter into egg yolk mixture. Place top of double boiler over boiling water. Upper pan should not touch water.

Cook and stir till butter melts and sauce starts to thicken. Continue stirring and adding butter, a few tablespoons at a time, till all butter has been used and sauce is smooth and thick. Remove from heat. Season to taste with salt; stir in tarragon. Serve over steaks. Makes 6 servings.

Elegant Beef Tenderloin

4 beef tenderloin steaks, cut
    ½ inch thick (1 pound)
1 tablespoon butter
¼ cup brandy
½ cup dairy sour cream
2 tablespoons catsup
¼ teaspoon salt
2 dashes Worcestershire sauce
2 drops bottled hot pepper
    sauce
Dash ground thyme

In skillet cook steaks in butter over medium heat to desired doneness, turning once. Allow 6 to 8 minutes total cooking time for medium-rare. Remove pan from heat; pour *half* of the brandy over cooked steaks. Transfer steaks to serving platter; keep warm.

Combine remaining brandy, sour cream, catsup, salt, Worcestershire sauce, hot pepper sauce, and thyme; add to same skillet. Heat, stirring constantly, just till mixture is heated through. *Do not boil.* Spoon some of the sauce over steaks; pass remaining sauce. Makes 4 servings.

Sirloin Especial

4 beef top loin steaks, cut
    ¾ inch thick
2 tablespoons butter *or*
    margarine
1 3-ounce can sliced mushrooms
¼ cup thinly sliced green onion
    with tops
1 tablespoon lemon juice
¼ teaspoon salt
¼ teaspoon dried basil,
    crushed
1 clove garlic, minced

Slash fat edge of steaks at 1-inch intervals. In skillet cook steaks in butter over medium heat to desired doneness, turning steaks once. Allow about 8 minutes total cooking time for rare, about 11 minutes for medium, or about 18 minutes for well done. Transfer to platter; keep warm.

In same skillet combine mushrooms, green onion, lemon juice, salt, basil, and garlic. Heat and stir till sauce is bubbly; serve with steaks. Makes 4 servings.

If it's raves you want, serve *Rice-Stuffed Steaks*. Thick, juicy top loin steaks
come to the table brushed with teriyaki sauce and filled with an onion-wild rice stuffing.

Steak au Poivre

**2 to 4 teaspoons whole black
    peppercorns**
**4 beef top loin steaks,
    cut 1 inch thick
    (about 2¼ pounds)**
**2 tablespoons butter *or*
    margarine
    Salt**
**¼ cup chopped shallots
    or green onion
    with tops**
**2 tablespoons butter *or*
    margarine**
⅓ cup water
**1 teaspoon instant beef
    bouillon granules**
3 tablespoons brandy

Coarsely crack the peppercorns with mortar and pestle or with spoon in metal mixing bowl. Slash fat edge of steaks at 1-inch intervals; place 1 steak on waxed paper. Sprinkle with *¼ to ½ teaspoon* of the cracked peppercorns; rub over meat and press in with heel of hand. Turn steak and repeat on other side. Repeat this procedure with the remaining three steaks.

In a 12-inch skillet melt the first 2 tablespoons butter or margarine. Cook steaks over medium-high heat to desired doneness, turning once. Allow 11 to 12 minutes total cooking time for medium doneness. Season steaks on both sides with a little salt. Transfer steaks to hot serving platter; keep hot.

In same skillet cook shallots in 2 tablespoons butter till tender but not brown, about 1 minute. Add water and bouillon granules; boil rapidly over high heat 1 minute, scraping up browned bits from pan. Stir in brandy; cook 1 minute more. Pour over steaks. Makes 4 servings.

Rice-Stuffed Steaks

1 6-ounce package long grain
and wild rice mix
1 beaten egg
¼ cup sliced green onion with
tops
6 beef top loin steaks,
cut 1 inch thick
¼ to ½ cup bottled teriyaki
sauce

Cook rice mix according to package directions, about 25 minutes. Cool slightly; stir in egg and onion.

Slash fat edge of steaks at 1-inch intervals. Cut a pocket in the side of each steak; stuff with rice mixture.

Place on cold rack of broiler pan. Broil 4 inches from heat to desired doneness, turning once. Allow 8 to 12 minutes total time for medium-rare. Brush often with teriyaki sauce. Trim with whole fresh mushrooms and watercress, if desired. Makes 6 servings.

Steak with Lobster Tail

4 beef top loin steaks, cut
1 inch thick
Salt
Pepper
4 4-ounce frozen lobster tails
¼ cup butter
2 teaspoons lemon juice
¼ teaspoon salt
Dash paprika

Slash fat edge of steaks at 1-inch intervals. In skillet cook steaks over medium-high heat to desired doneness; turn occasionally. Allow 9 to 10 minutes total time for rare or 11 to 12 minutes for medium. Season with salt and pepper.

Meanwhile, drop frozen lobster tails in boiling salted water to cover. Return to boiling; reduce heat. Simmer 8 minutes; drain. Snip along each side of thin undershell; remove undershell. Remove meat from shells; cut in chunks. Return to shells; place one atop each steak.

In saucepan melt butter; stir in lemon juice, salt, and paprika. Spoon over lobster. Makes 4 servings.

Broiling Beef Steaks

Thickness of Steak	Rare	Medium	Well Done
	(approximate total time in minutes)		
1 inch	8 to 10	12 to 14	18 to 20
1½ inch	14 to 16	18 to 20	25 to 30
2 inch	20 to 25	30 to 35	40 to 45

Choose a beef porterhouse, T-bone, top loin, sirloin, or tenderloin steak cut 1 to 2 inches thick. Without cutting into the meat, slash the fat edge at 1-inch intervals. Place steak on cold rack of broiler pan.

Broil 1- to 1½-inch-thick steaks so surface of meat is 3 inches from heat. Broil thicker cuts 4 to 5 inches from heat. (Check range instruction booklet.) Broil on one side for about half of the time indicated in chart for desired doneness. Season with salt and pepper, if desired. Turn with tongs and broil for remaining time. Season again.

Doneness test: Slit center; note inside color: red—rare; pink—medium; gray—well done.

Beef Steaks Wellington

8 5-ounce beef tenderloin steaks
   Cooking oil
   Salt
   Pepper
½ pound ground beef sirloin
1 teaspoon snipped parsley
¼ teaspoon garlic salt
   Dash pepper
8 frozen patty shells, thawed
·1 slightly beaten egg white
3 egg yolks
½ cup butter *or* margarine,
   melted
2 tablespoons lemon juice
2 tablespoons hot water
¼ teaspoon salt
1 teaspoon snipped parsley
⅛ teaspoon dried tarragon,
   crushed

Brush steaks with oil; sprinkle with a little salt and pepper. In hot skillet brown steaks 5 minutes on *each* side. Transfer to plate; chill.

Combine ground sirloin, 1 teaspoon parsley, ¼ teaspoon garlic salt, and dash pepper. Divide mixture into 8 portions; spoon a mound atop each steak.

Roll each patty shell to a 9x5-inch rectangle. Place steaks, ground sirloin sides down, on pastry rectangles. Fold pastry over meat; seal. Place seam side down in shallow pan. If desired, top with cutouts from an additional rolled-out patty shell; chill at least 30 minutes.

Before cooking, brush pastry with egg white. Bake at 450° to desired doneness. Allow 18 minutes for rare, 20 minutes for medium-rare, or 22 minutes for medium.

Meanwhile, in top of double boiler (not over water) beat egg yolks with wire whisk till smooth but not fluffy. Add melted butter, lemon juice, hot water, and ¼ teaspoon salt. Place over hot, not boiling, water; upper pan should not touch water. Cook and beat till sauce begins to thicken, about 5 minutes. Stir in 1 teaspoon parsley and tarragon. If sauce starts to separate, add a small amount of cold water and beat. Serve sauce with steaks. Makes 8 servings.

Tenderloin Steaks with Royal Mushroom Sauce

6 beef tenderloin steaks, cut
   1 inch thick
2 tablespoons butter
   Salt
   Pepper
½ cup chopped fresh mushrooms
¼ cup sliced green onion with
   tops
4 teaspoons cornstarch
1 cup Burgundy
½ cup water
2 tablespoons snipped parsley
1 teaspoon salt
   Dash pepper

In skillet, cook steaks in butter over medium-high heat to desired doneness, turning occasionally. Allow 9 to 10 minutes total cooking time for rare; or 11 to 12 minutes for medium. Season with a little salt and pepper. Transfer steaks to serving platter; keep hot.

In same skillet, cook mushrooms and green onion till tender but not brown. Blend in cornstarch. Stir in Burgundy, water, parsley, 1 teaspoon salt, and dash pepper; cook and stir till thickened and bubbly. Cook and stir 1 minute more. Serve sauce over steaks. Makes 6 servings.

Wine-Sauced Steak Sandwiches

4 slices French bread,
   sliced diagonally
¼ cup butter, softened
4 beef top loin steaks, cut
   ½ inch thick
   (about 1½ pounds)
2 tablespoons butter
   Salt
   Pepper
¼ cup port
½ cup whipping cream

Spread bread on both sides with the ¼ cup butter. In skillet toast bread till golden brown. Transfer to serving plates.

Slash fat edge of steaks at 1-inch intervals. In same skillet, cook steaks in 2 tablespoons butter to desired doneness, turning once. Allow about 10 minutes total cooking time for medium-rare. Season with salt and pepper. Place steaks atop toasted bread slices; keep warm.

Add port to skillet; stir to blend with pan drippings. Add cream; cook and stir till thickened and bubbly. Season with salt; pour sauce over steaks. Makes 4 servings.

Grilling Steaks Outdoors

Thickness of Steak	Temperature of Coals	Open Grill		Covered Grill	
		Rare	Medium	Rare	Medium
		(approximate total time in minutes)			
1 inch	Medium-hot	12 to 18	15 to 20	8 to 10	10 to 15
1½ inch	Medium-hot	18 to 20	20 to 25	10 to 15	15 to 18
	Medium	20 to 25	25 to 30	15 to 18	18 to 22

Choose sirloin, porterhouse, or T-bone steaks. Slash the fat edge at about 1-inch intervals to keep steaks flat on grill. To estimate temperature of coals, hold hand, palm side down, about *4 inches* above coals. Count seconds "one thousand one, one thousand two," and so on. When you can hold your hand comfortably over the coals for 2 to 3 seconds, they have a temperature of *medium-hot;* 3 to 4 seconds indicates *medium.* Grill steaks for about half of the given time. Flip steaks using tongs and pancake turner (piercing with fork wastes good meat juices); grill till desired doneness.

Mushroom-Sauced Tournedos

6 **6-ounce beef tenderloin**
   steaks, cut 1 inch thick
2 **4½-ounce jars whole**
   mushrooms, drained
2 **tablespoons butter** *or*
   margarine
   Salt
   Pepper
⅓ **cup Burgundy**
½ **cup whipping cream**

Trim any excess fat from steaks. In skillet cook mushrooms in butter; push to one side. In same skillet, cook steaks over medium heat to desired doneness, turning once. Allow 10 minutes total cooking time for rare. Season with a little salt and pepper. Transfer to serving platter; keep warm.

Add Burgundy to skillet; stir to loosen crusty bits from bottom of pan. Add cream; cook and stir over low heat till sauce is slightly thickened, about 4 minutes. Serve mushroom sauce over steaks. Makes 6 servings.

Swank Steak

1 **2-pound beef porterhouse**
   steak, 1½ inches thick
½ **cup chopped onion**
1 **large clove garlic, minced**
3 **tablespoons butter** *or*
   margarine
   Dash salt
   Dash pepper
   Dash celery salt
¼ **cup Burgundy**
2 **tablespoons soy sauce**
1 **cup sliced fresh mushrooms**

Slash fat edge of steak at 1-inch intervals. Slicing from fat side, cut pocket in steak, cutting almost to bone.

Cook onion and garlic in *1 tablespoon* of the butter; sprinkle with salt, pepper, and celery salt. Stuff mixture into pocket of steak; use wooden picks to skewer closed, if necessary. Mix Burgundy and soy sauce; brush over steak.

Grill steak over *medium-hot* coals (or broil 3 to 4 inches from heat source), turning once. Allow 25 to 30 minutes total cooking time for rare. Brush occasionally with sauce.

Meanwhile, in small skillet cook mushrooms in remaining 2 tablespoons butter till tender, 3 to 5 minutes; spoon over steak. Slice steak across grain. Serves 4 to 6.

Steaks that Cost Less

Budget Steak Diane

1 pound beef round steak, cut
    ½ inch thick
¼ cup dry sherry
2 tablespoons water
1 tablespoon snipped chives
1 tablespoon bottled steak sauce
½ teaspoon dry mustard
2 tablespoons cooking oil
1 3-ounce can sliced mushrooms
¼ cup brandy

Cut meat into 4 serving-size portions; place in shallow dish. Combine sherry, water, chives, steak sauce, and dry mustard; pour over steak. Cover and refrigerate for several hours or overnight. Spoon marinade over occasionally.

Drain steak; reserve marinade. Pat steak dry with paper toweling. Cook, 2 pieces at a time, in hot oil about 2 minutes; turn and cook 2 minutes more. Transfer to platter; keep warm. Repeat with remaining 2 pieces. Add reserved marinade and mushrooms to skillet. Bring to boiling; pour over steak. Warm brandy in ladle. Ignite; carefully pour over meat. Serve when flame subsides. Makes 4 servings.

Cheese-Stuffed Beef Rounds

2 pounds beef round steak, cut
    ½ inch thick
¼ cup all-purpose flour
1 teaspoon salt
⅛ teaspoon pepper
3 ribs celery, chopped (1 cup)
1 medium onion, chopped (½ cup)
3 sprigs parsley, snipped
2 tablespoons butter
1 cup shredded sharp American
    cheese (4 ounces)
½ cup soft bread crumbs
2 tablespoons cooking oil
1 cup water
1½ teaspoons instant beef
    bouillon granules
½ teaspoon dry mustard
¼ teaspoon dried thyme, crushed
¼ cup cold water
2 tablespoons all-purpose flour
½ teaspoon Kitchen Bouquet
    (optional)

Cut steak into 6 serving-size pieces. Combine the ¼ cup flour, salt, and pepper; with meat mallet, pound flour mixture into meat, pounding each piece to about a 5-inch square.

Cook celery, onion, and parsley in butter till tender but not brown; remove from heat. Stir in cheese and bread crumbs. Spread *about ⅓ cup* of the cheese mixture over each steak; roll up as for jelly roll. Secure steak rolls with wooden picks or tie with string.

In 10-inch skillet slowly brown steak rolls on all sides in hot oil; drain off excess fat. Combine 1 cup water, beef bouillon granules, dry mustard, and thyme; pour over steak rolls in skillet. Cover and cook over low heat till meat is tender, 1 to 1¼ hours.

Transfer meat to serving platter; keep warm. Skim excess fat from pan juices. Blend ¼ cup cold water with 2 tablespoons flour; stir into pan juices. Cook and stir till thickened and bubbly; stir in Kitchen Bouquet, if desired. Serve gravy with steak rolls. Remove picks or string from meat before serving. Makes 6 servings.

Steaks Bertrand

6 beef cubed steaks
⅔ cup dry red wine
1 6-ounce can whole mushrooms
¼ cup snipped parsley
    Dash garlic powder
6 tablespoons butter *or*
    margarine
3 slices Swiss cheese, halved

Place steaks in plastic bag; set in deep bowl. Mix wine, mushrooms, parsley, and garlic powder. Pour over meat in bag; close. Marinate ½ hour at room temperature or 2 hours in refrigerator. Drain; reserve marinade.

In skillet, melt butter. Cook meat, half at a time, in butter, about 2 minutes; turn. Cook 2 minutes more; transfer to blazer pan of chafing dish. Repeat. Add reserved marinade to skillet; bring to boiling. Pour over meat. Top with cheese. Cover; place chafing dish on stand. Heat to melt cheese, 2 minutes. Serve sauce with meat. Serves 6.

You can save your food budget and still please family and friends with *Budget Steak Diane*.
This economical version of the classic dish uses tenderized round steak and canned mushrooms.

Rolled Beef Italian-Style

1 1½-pound beef round steak, cut
    about ½ inch thick
1 beaten egg
½ pound ground pork
4 ounces ground fully cooked ham
    (¾ cup)
¼ cup grated Parmesan cheese
    (1 ounce)
¼ cup snipped parsley
1 tablespoon olive oil
1 tablespoon butter *or* margarine
1 large onion, chopped (¾ cup)
1 clove garlic, minced
¼ cup cognac *or* brandy
½ cup dry red wine
1 cup beef broth
¼ cup tomato paste
1 teaspoon dried oregano,
    crushed
    Hot cooked noodles

With meat mallet, pound a generous amount of salt and pepper into steak till meat is ¼ inch thick. Combine egg, pork, ham, Parmesan, and parsley. Spread pork mixture evenly over steak; roll up meat as for jelly roll. Press seams together; tie securely with string or skewer.

In skillet, brown meat roll on all sides in mixture of hot olive oil and butter. Add onion and garlic. Cook till onion is tender but not brown; remove from heat.

Add cognac to skillet and ignite. When flame has subsided, return skillet to heat. Add wine; simmer till wine is nearly evaporated. Stir in beef broth, tomato paste, and oregano. Cover and simmer 45 minutes; baste occasionally.

Remove meat from skillet; slice and arrange atop hot cooked noodles on serving platter. (Center of meat roll will have a pink color when sliced.) Skim fat from sauce in skillet; pour sauce over all. Makes 6 to 8 servings.

Vegetable-Stuffed Cubed Steaks

6 beef cubed steaks
    Salt
    Pepper
¼ cup water
¼ teaspoon salt
1½ cups shredded carrot
¾ cup finely chopped onion
¾ cup finely chopped green
    pepper
¾ cup finely chopped celery
⅓ cup French salad dressing
6 slices bacon

Sprinkle meat with a little salt and pepper; set aside. In saucepan bring water and ¼ teaspoon salt to boiling; add vegetables. Simmer, covered, till vegetables are crisp-tender, 7 to 8 minutes; drain. Stir in *2 tablespoons* of the salad dressing. Place *about ⅓ cup* of the vegetable mixture on each steak; roll up as for jelly roll. Wrap a bacon slice around each meat roll; secure with wooden picks.

Place meat rolls on cold rack of broiler pan. Broil 3 to 4 inches from heat for 20 to 25 minutes; turn rolls about every 5 minutes and brush with remaining salad dressing. (*Or,* place meat rolls on grill. Cook over *hot* coals 20 to 25 minutes; turn rolls about every 5 minutes and brush with remaining salad dressing.) Remove picks. Makes 6 servings.

Bavarian Supper

4 beef cubed steaks
    (1 to 1¼ pounds)
1 tablespoon cooking oil
⅓ cup chopped onion
2½ cups water
2 envelopes mushroom gravy mix
2 tablespoons brown sugar
2 tablespoons vinegar
1 teaspoon caraway seed
3 cups coarsely shredded cabbage
2 medium potatoes, peeled and
    cubed (2 cups)

In large skillet, quickly brown steaks on both sides in hot oil. Add onion; cook till onion is almost tender, about 5 minutes. Combine water, mushroom gravy mix, brown sugar, vinegar, and caraway; pour over steaks in skillet. Cover; simmer for 15 minutes. Skim off excess fat.

Meanwhile, cook cabbage with potatoes, covered, in boiling salted water till tender, 5 to 7 minutes; drain. Spoon cabbage and potatoes onto serving platter; arrange steaks atop vegetables. Serve with gravy. Makes 4 servings.

Bacon-Pepper-Stuffed Round Steak

1 small green pepper, cut in
    strips
6 slices bacon
1 3-pound boneless beef top
    round steak, cut 1½ inches
    thick
1 8-ounce can tomato sauce
¼ cup packed brown sugar
¼ cup red wine vinegar
1 teaspoon salt
1 bay leaf
¼ cup all-purpose flour
    Hot cooked rice
    (optional)

Cook green pepper in boiling, salted water 5 minutes. Drain; set aside. In skillet, cook bacon till nearly done; drain bacon, reserving drippings in skillet.

Using a sharp knife, make a deep horizontal slit in steak. Stuff steak with green pepper and bacon, breaking up bacon to fit pocket. Brown meat on both sides in hot bacon drippings. Transfer meat to a 12x7½x2-inch baking dish.

In same skillet, combine tomato sauce, brown sugar, red wine vinegar, salt, and bay leaf. Heat and stir till sugar dissolves. Pour *half* of the sauce over meat; reserve remainder. Cook meat, covered, at 325° till tender, about 1½ hours, occasionally spooning pan juices over meat.

Remove meat to serving platter; keep warm. Pour pan juices into measuring cup; skim off fat. Add water to juices to make 2¼ cups. Blend reserved sauce with flour; stir into pan juices. Cook and stir till thickened and bubbly.

Slice meat. Spoon some gravy over meat; pass remaining. Serve with rice, if desired. Makes 6 to 8 servings.

Roulades of Beef with Crab Stuffing

2 pounds beef top round steak,
    cut ¼ inch thick
1 beaten egg
¼ cup milk
1 tablespoon lemon juice
½ teaspoon Worcestershire sauce
¼ teaspoon salt
1 7½-ounce can crab meat,
    drained, flaked, and
    cartilage removed
½ cup fine dry bread crumbs
2 tablespoons snipped parsley
3 tablespoons cooking oil
¾ cup dry white wine
1 teaspoon instant beef
    bouillon granules
½ teaspoon salt
1 clove garlic, minced
1 bay leaf
2 tablespoons cornstarch

Cut beef into 12 rectangles; pound to ⅛-inch thickness. Mix egg, milk, lemon juice, Worcestershire, and ¼ teaspoon salt. Stir in crab meat, crumbs, and *1 tablespoon parsley*.

Place *1 heaping tablespoon* crab filling at one end of each piece of meat; roll as for jelly roll. Secure with wooden picks. In skillet, brown rolls, a few at a time, on all sides in hot oil; transfer to 12x7½x2-inch baking dish; repeat.

To juices in skillet stir in wine, bouillon granules, ½ teaspoon salt, garlic, bay leaf, remaining 1 tablespoon parsley, and ¾ cup water. Bring to boiling; scrape pan to mix in crusty bits. Pour over meat rolls; cover tightly with foil. Bake at 350° till tender, about 1 hour.

Transfer meat rolls to serving platter; keep hot. Strain pan juices into measuring cup; skim off excess fat. Add water, if necessary, to make 1½ cups. Pour juices into saucepan. Stir in 2 to 3 tablespoons additional dry white wine, if desired. Blend cornstarch with 2 tablespoons cold water. Add to pan juices; cook and stir till thickened and bubbly. Pour some sauce over meat; pass remainder. Serves 6.

Cubed Steaks Parmesan

1 egg
    Dash pepper
¼ cup finely crushed saltine
    crackers (6 or 7 crackers)
¼ cup grated Parmesan cheese
5 beef cubed steaks (about 4
    ounces each)
2 tablespoons cooking oil
1 8-ounce can pizza sauce

Beat together egg, pepper, and 1 tablespoon water. Combine crumbs and *2 tablespoons* of the cheese. Dip steaks in egg mixture, then in crumbs. In skillet, brown the steaks in hot oil. Drain off fat. Pour in pizza sauce. Cover; reduce heat. Simmer 20 minutes, adding a little water, if necessary, to keep the sauce from sticking. Sprinkle with the remaining 2 tablespoons cheese. Makes 5 servings.

Spinach-Stuffed Flank Steak lets you serve a less-costly beef cut without sacrificing flavor. Baked in a tomato-wine sauce, these flavorful meat rolls boast a cheesy spinach filling.

Saucy Steak Sandwich

1 8-ounce can tomato sauce
3 tablespoons bottled steak
   sauce
2 tablespoons brown sugar
1 tablespoon cooking oil
6 slices French bread, cut
   ½ inch thick
1 pound beef round steak, cut
   ¼ inch thick
   Instant unseasoned meat
   tenderizer
   Shortening
   Pepper

In small saucepan combine tomato sauce, steak sauce, brown sugar, and oil. Bring sauce to boiling; keep warm.

Toast French bread slices on both sides. Cut steak into 6 pieces; pound each piece to ⅛-inch thickness. Apply tenderizer to meat according to label directions.

In lightly greased hot skillet, cook meat 2 minutes. Turn; cook 2 minutes more. Sprinkle with pepper. To serve, dip one side of each toast slice quickly into sauce. Top each slice with a steak. Spoon on additional sauce. Makes 6 servings.

Spinach-Stuffed Flank Steak

2 1-pound beef flank steaks
1 beaten egg
1 10-ounce package frozen chopped spinach, cooked and drained
½ cup shredded sharp American cheese (2 ounces)
½ teaspoon ground sage
¼ teaspoon salt
    Dash pepper
¾ cup soft bread crumbs
2 tablespoons cooking oil
1 8-ounce can tomato sauce
½ cup dry red wine
½ cup chopped onion
1 clove garlic, minced
2 tablespoons all-purpose flour

Pound each steak with meat mallet to ¼-inch thickness; set aside. Combine egg, spinach, cheese, sage, salt, and pepper; stir in soft bread crumbs. Spread spinach filling over steaks. Starting from narrow side, roll up each steak as for jelly roll; tie with string.

In large skillet, brown steak rolls on all sides in hot oil; transfer rolls to a 10x6x2-inch baking dish. Combine tomato sauce, wine, onion, and garlic; pour over meat. Cover with foil; bake at 350° till tender, about 1½ hours.

Transfer meat to serving platter; keep warm. Pour pan juices into measuring cup; add water to equal 1¾ cups. Pour juice mixture into a 1-quart saucepan. Combine ¼ cup cold water and flour; stir into pan juices. Cook and stir over medium heat till thickened and bubbly.

To serve, remove string from meat rolls; slice meat rolls. Pass sauce. Makes 8 servings.

Mexican Flank Steak

2 1-pound beef flank steaks
½ teaspoon salt
⅛ teaspoon garlic salt
⅛ teaspoon pepper
1 15-ounce can tamales in sauce
1 teaspoon instant beef bouillon granules
¼ cup boiling water
1 8-ounce can tomato sauce
    Dash bottled hot pepper sauce
    Shredded Monterey Jack cheese

Pound meat on both sides; sprinkle with salt, garlic salt, and pepper. Unwrap tamales; place in bowl. Break up slightly with fork; spread over steaks. Roll up as for jelly rolls; tie closed. Place in shallow baking pan. Dissolve bouillon in boiling water; mix with tomato sauce and hot pepper sauce. Pour over meat. Bake at 350° for 1¼ to 1½ hours, basting often. Remove strings. Top meat with cheese. Serves 6.

Crockery cooker directions: Prepare steak rolls as above. Place in electric slow crockery cooker. Dissolve bouillon granules in boiling water; combine with tomato sauce and hot pepper sauce. Pour over meat. Cover; cook on low-heat setting 8 to 10 hours. Transfer meat rolls to serving platter; remove strings. Keep meat rolls warm.

Pour cooking liquid into saucepan; skim off excess fat. Blend 2 tablespoons cold water with 4 teaspoons cornstarch; stir into liquid. Cook and stir till thickened and bubbly. Spoon over meat; sprinkle cheese atop.

London Broil

1 1- to 1¼-pound beef flank steak
⅓ cup cooking oil
1 teaspoon vinegar
1 small clove garlic, minced
    Salt
    Freshly ground pepper

Score steak on both sides. Place steak in clear plastic bag; set in deep bowl. Combine oil, vinegar, and garlic; pour over steak. Close bag. Let stand at room temperature 2 to 3 hours, turning bag several times.

Remove steak from marinade; place on cold rack of broiler pan. Broil 3 inches from heat 4 to 5 minutes; sprinkle with salt and pepper. Turn; broil 4 to 5 minutes more for medium rare. Sprinkle with salt and pepper. Carve in very thin slices diagonally across grain. Makes 4 or 5 servings.

Oven Swiss Steak

1½ **pounds beef round steak, cut**
    ¾ **inch thick**
¼ **cup all-purpose flour**
1 **teaspoon salt**
2 **tablespoons shortening**
1 **16-ounce can tomatoes, cut up**
½ **cup finely chopped celery**
½ **cup finely chopped carrot**
½ **teaspoon Worcestershire sauce**

Cut meat into 6 serving-size portions. Combine flour and salt; pound *2 tablespoons* of the mixture into meat.

    Brown meat on both sides in hot shortening. Transfer meat to a 12x7½x2-inch baking dish. Blend remaining 2 tablespoons flour mixture into pan drippings. Stir in undrained tomatoes, celery, carrot, and Worcestershire. Cook and stir till thickened and bubbly; pour over meat.

    Bake, covered, at 350° till tender, about 1 hour and 20 minutes. Makes 6 servings.

Deviled Swiss Steak

1 **3-pound beef round steak, cut**
    1 inch thick
2 **teaspoons dry mustard**
1½ **teaspoons salt**
¼ **teaspoon pepper**
2 **tablespoons cooking oil**
1 **4-ounce can mushroom stems**
    and pieces
1 **tablespoon Worcestershire**
    sauce

Trim excess fat from meat; cut meat in half crosswise for easier handling. Mix dry mustard, salt, and pepper; pound seasonings into meat. In heavy 12-inch skillet quickly brown steak on both sides in hot oil; drain off excess fat.

    Drain mushrooms, reserving liquid; add water, if needed, to equal ½ cup. Add mushroom liquid and Worcestershire to skillet. Cover; simmer till meat is tender, 1¼ to 1½ hours.

    During last few minutes, add mushrooms; heat through. Skim fat from pan juices before serving. Makes 8 servings.

Chicken-Fried Round Steak

1½ **pounds beef round steak, cut**
    ½ **inch thick**
1 **beaten egg**
1 **tablespoon milk**
1 **cup finely crushed saltine**
    crackers (28 crackers)
½ **teaspoon salt**
¼ **teaspoon pepper**
¼ **cup cooking oil**

Pound steak to ¼-inch thickness; cut in 6 serving-size pieces. Blend egg and milk; combine cracker crumbs, salt, and pepper. Dip meat in egg mixture, then in crumbs.

    In 12-inch skillet slowly brown meat in hot oil, turning once. Cover tightly; cook over low heat till meat is tender, 45 to 60 minutes. Makes 6 servings.

Marinated Beef Broil

½ **cup pineapple juice**
1 **envelope meat marinade**
2 **tablespoons lemon juice**
¼ **teaspoon dried basil, crushed**
1 **clove garlic, minced**
1 **2-pound beef round steak, cut**
    1 inch thick
½ **cup water**

Stir pineapple juice into marinade; stir in lemon juice, basil, and garlic. Trim any excess fat from steak; place in shallow pan. Pour marinade over. Pierce steak surfaces deeply with long-tined fork; let stand 15 minutes, turning often. Drain; reserve marinade.

    Place steak on cold rack of broiler pan. Broil 3 inches from heat 10 minutes; turn, brushing with some of the reserved marinade. Broil to desired doneness, 8 to 10 minutes more. Stir water into reserved marinade; heat to boiling. Reduce heat; simmer 5 minutes. Pass with steak. Serves 6.

Chopped carrots, celery, and tomatoes add flavor as well as color to *Oven Swiss Steak*.
Put six baking potatoes alongside the meat to share the oven heat and complete the dinner.

Start with round steak for *Italian Braciole*. Fill the seasoned meat with chopped onion, then roll up and bake in a spicy tomato sauce flavored by mushrooms and olives.

Barbecued Steak Sandwiches

2 1-pound beef flank steaks
   Instant unseasoned meat
    tenderizer
2 tablespoons prepared
   horseradish
⅓ cup chopped onion
⅓ cup chopped celery
2 tablespoons butter *or*
   margarine, melted
½ teaspoon seasoned salt
1 cup dairy sour cream
12 slices French bread, toasted
   and buttered
   Paprika

Score steaks on both sides. Use tenderizer according to label directions. Spread one side of each steak with horseradish. Thoroughly mix together the chopped onion, chopped celery, melted butter, and seasoned salt. Spread over horseradish side of steaks. Roll up as for jelly roll; fasten with skewers and tie with string.

Balance meat rolls, crosswise, on spit rod; secure with holding forks. Attach spit. Center drip pan under meat, placing *medium* coals on both sides of pan. Turn on motor. Roast over *medium* coals till done, about 45 minutes. Let stand a few minutes; remove strings and skewers.

Heat sour cream over low heat; *do not boil*. To serve, thinly slice meat rolls. For each sandwich, arrange a few meat slices over 2 slices bread; top with a little warm sour cream. Sprinkle with paprika. Makes 6 servings.

Italian Braciole

2 pounds beef round steak, cut
    ¼ inch thick
Salt
Pepper
½ cup chopped onion
¼ cup chili sauce
¼ cup condensed beef
    broth
1 3-ounce can sliced
    mushrooms
2 tablespoons chopped green
    pepper
2 tablespoons sliced
    pimiento-stuffed
    green olives
1 teaspoon sugar
1 teaspoon Worcestershire
    sauce
¼ teaspoon dried oregano,
    crushed
⅛ teaspoon garlic powder
⅛ teaspoon pepper
    Hot cooked spaghetti
½ cup cold water
3 tablespoons all-purpose flour

Cut steak into 6 rectangular pieces; pound each piece flat. Season with a little salt and pepper. Spread onion over meat to within ½ inch of edge. Roll up each piece as for jelly roll; secure meat rolls with wooden picks. Place meat rolls, seam side down, in a 10x6x2-inch baking dish.

Combine chili sauce, condensed beef broth, undrained mushrooms, chopped green pepper, sliced olives, sugar, Worcestershire sauce, oregano, garlic powder, and ⅛ teaspoon pepper. Pour over meat rolls. Bake, covered, at 350° till meat is tender, about 1¼ hours.

Arrange meat rolls atop spaghetti on serving platter; keep warm. Pour pan juices into measuring cup; skim off excess fat. Add enough water to juices to make 1½ cups; pour into saucepan. Blend ½ cup cold water with flour; add to juices. Cook and stir till thickened and bubbly. Spoon some sauce over meat; pass remaining. Makes 6 servings.

Shaker-Style Steak

2 pounds beef round steak, cut
    ¾ inch thick
¼ cup all-purpose flour
    Salt
    Pepper
¾ cup catsup
¾ cup water
¾ cup finely chopped onion
    (1 large)
¾ cup finely chopped carrot
    (1 large)
½ cup finely chopped celery
    (1 large rib)
¼ cup finely chopped green
    pepper
1 tablespoon vinegar

Trim fat from steak; reserve trimmings. In skillet, cook trimmings till 2 tablespoons fat accumulate; discard trimmings. Pound flour into steak; brown on both sides in hot fat. Spoon off excess fat. Season meat with salt and pepper.

Combine catsup, water, onion, carrot, celery, green pepper and vinegar. Pour over meat; reduce heat. Cover; simmer till meat and vegetables are tender, about 1 hour. Serve meat with vegetable sauce. Makes 6 to 8 servings.

Crockery cooker directions: Trim fat from meat. (Do not pound or coat with flour.) Cut meat into 6 to 8 pieces; set aside. Place chopped vegetables in electric slow crockery cooker. Place meat atop; sprinkle with salt and pepper.

Mix *only* ½ *cup* catsup and *only* ⅓ *cup* water with vinegar; pour over meat. Cover; cook on low-heat setting 8 to 10 hours. Remove meat. Pour vegetables and cooking liquid into saucepan; skim off excess fat. Return meat to cooker.

Blend ½ cup cold water with 2 tablespoons all-purpose flour. Stir into vegetables. Cook and stir till thickened and bubbly. Transfer meat to serving platter. Spoon some gravy over meat; pass remaining. Serves 6 to 8.

3 Always-Popular Ground Beef

A traditional fondness for beef tempered by watch-the-budget economics gives ground beef an important role in family meal plans. Use the recipes in this chapter to rediscover favorite ways of serving this versatile meat by itself in burgers, meat loaves, and meatballs. Or include it as a combination ingredient in one-dish meals, pizzas, and sandwiches.

Ground beef combines with traditionally American cornmeal for *Beef-Filled Corn Bread Squares* (see recipe, page 55). Chili peppers season the tomato sauce that is spooned atop.

Meat Loaves and Meatballs

Everyday Meat Loaf

2 beaten eggs
¾ cup milk
½ cup fine dry bread crumbs
¼ cup finely chopped onion
2 tablespoons snipped parsley
1 teaspoon salt
½ teaspoon ground sage
⅛ teaspoon pepper
1½ pounds ground beef
¼ cup catsup
2 tablespoons brown sugar
1 teaspoon dry mustard

Combine eggs and milk; stir in crumbs, onion, parsley, salt, sage, and pepper. Add ground beef; mix well. Pat into a 5½-cup ring mold; unmold in shallow baking pan. Bake at 350° for 50 minutes. (Or pat mixture into 8½x4½x2½-inch loaf pan; bake for 1¼ hours.) Spoon off excess fat. Combine catsup, brown sugar, and dry mustard; spread over meat loaf. Return to oven for 10 minutes. Makes 6 servings.

Microwave cooking directions: Prepare meat mixture as directed above; pat into a 5½-cup ring mold. Invert into a 9- or 10-inch glass pie plate; *remove mold*. (Do not use a loaf pan.) Cover with waxed paper. Cook in a countertop microwave oven till meat is done, 12 to 13 minutes; give dish a quarter turn every 3 minutes. Spoon off excess fat. Combine catsup, brown sugar, and mustard; spread over meat loaf. Let stand 5 minutes. Transfer to serving platter.

Stroganoff Meat Loaves

2 beaten eggs
1⅓ cups milk
1 cup quick-cooking rolled oats
¾ cup chopped onion
1 tablespoon Worcestershire
    sauce
2¼ teaspoons salt
½ teaspoon pepper
3 pounds ground beef
3 4-ounce cans chopped
    mushrooms, drained
1 cup dairy sour cream
½ teaspoon salt
4 large whole fresh mushrooms,
    quartered (optional)

In large bowl beat together the eggs and milk; stir in oats, onion, Worcestershire, the 2¼ teaspoons salt, and pepper. Add ground beef and mix well. Pat about one-fourth of the meat mixture into *each* of two 8½x4½x2½-inch loaf pans, making a shallow depression through the centers.

In small bowl combine chopped mushrooms, sour cream, and the ½ teaspoon salt. Divide between the meat loaves, spreading half in the depression in each loaf. Cover with remaining meat mixture, pressing firmly to seal edges.

Bake at 350° till done, 1 to 1¼ hours. Let stand 5 to 10 minutes before removing from pans. If desired, trim top of loaves with quartered whole mushrooms. Makes 2 meat loaves, 6 or 7 servings each.

Berry-Glazed Loaves

1 beaten egg
⅓ cup milk
⅓ cup quick-cooking rolled oats
2 tablespoons finely chopped
    onion
½ teaspoon salt
    Dash pepper
1 pound ground beef
¼ pound bulk pork sausage
1 8-ounce can whole cranberry
    sauce
3 tablespoons brown sugar
2 teaspoons lemon juice

In bowl beat together egg and milk; stir in oats, onion, salt, and pepper. Add beef and sausage; mix well. Shape into five 4x2-inch loaves. Place in 13x9x2-inch baking pan so loaves do not touch each other.

Bake at 350° for 30 minutes; drain off excess fat. Combine cranberry sauce, brown sugar, and lemon juice; spoon over loaves. Bake 15 minutes more. Makes 5 servings.

Sicilian Meat Roll

2 beaten eggs
½ cup tomato juice
¾ cup soft bread crumbs
2 tablespoons snipped parsley
½ teaspoon dried oregano, crushed
¼ teaspoon salt
¼ teaspoon pepper
1 clove garlic, minced
2 pounds ground beef
4 to 6 ounces thinly sliced boiled ham
1 6-ounce package sliced mozzarella cheese

In a bowl combine the eggs and tomato juice. Stir in the bread crumbs, parsley, oregano, salt, pepper, and garlic. Add ground beef; mix well. On waxed paper or foil pat meat to a 10x8-inch rectangle. Arrange ham slices atop meat, leaving a small margin around edges.

Reserve 1 slice of cheese. Tear up remaining cheese; sprinkle over ham. Starting from short end, carefully roll up meat, using paper to lift; seal edges and ends. Place roll, seam side down, in 13x9x2-inch baking pan.

Bake at 350° till done, about 1¼ hours. (Center of roll will be pink due to ham.) Cut reserved cheese slice into 4 triangles; overlap atop meat. Return to oven till cheese melts, about 2 minutes. Makes 8 servings.

Meat Loaf Florentine

1 10-ounce package frozen chopped spinach, thawed
2 beaten eggs
½ cup milk
1½ cups soft bread crumbs (2 slices)
2 tablespoons soy sauce
1½ teaspoons salt
¼ teaspoon bottled hot pepper sauce
2 pounds ground beef
Mushroom Sauce

Drain spinach well; combine with eggs and milk. Stir in bread crumbs, soy, salt, and hot pepper sauce. Add beef; mix well. Pat into 9x5x3-inch loaf pan. Bake at 350° for 1½ hours. Serve with Mushroom Sauce. Makes 8 servings.

Mushroom Sauce: In saucepan combine one 3-ounce can chopped mushrooms, undrained, and 1 tablespoon all-purpose flour. Stir in 1 cup dairy sour cream and 2 table-spoons snipped chives. Cook and stir just till thickened. *Do not boil.*

Crockery cooker directions: Prepare meat mixture as above. Shape into round loaf slightly smaller in diameter than electric slow crockery cooker. Crisscross two 15x2-inch strips of foil (double thickness) across bottom and up sides of cooker. Place loaf atop, not touching sides. Cover; cook on high-heat setting for 4 hours. Lift loaf from cooker using foil strips. Serve with Mushroom Sauce.

Applesauce-Beef Loaf

1 beaten egg
1 cup soft bread crumbs
1 8½-ounce can applesauce
2 tablespoons finely chopped onion
2 teaspoons prepared mustard
1 teaspoon dried celery flakes
½ teaspoon salt
Dash pepper
1½ pounds ground beef
1 tablespoon brown sugar
1 tablespoon vinegar
¼ teaspoon ground allspice

In a bowl combine the egg, bread crumbs, ½ *cup* of the applesauce, onion, *1 teaspoon* of the prepared mustard, celery flakes, salt, and pepper. Add ground beef, mix well. Shape into a round loaf in a shallow baking pan. Make a de-pression in top of loaf.

Combine the remaining ½ cup applesauce and 1 teaspoon mustard; stir in the brown sugar, vinegar, and allspice. Spoon into depression. Bake at 350° for 50 to 60 minutes. Makes 6 to 8 servings.

Mozzarella cheese and sliced ham are the extra-special fillings in *Sicilian Meat Roll*.
Pat the ground beef mixture on waxed paper to make it easier to roll for the pinwheel effect.

Meat Loaf Puff

  1 beaten egg
¾ cup milk
1½ cups soft bread crumbs
    (2 slices)
  1 medium onion, chopped (½ cup)
1½ teaspoons salt
⅛ teaspoon pepper
1½ pounds ground beef
  2 medium tomatoes, peeled
  6 slices American cheese
  3 egg whites
¾ cup all-purpose flour
  1 cup dairy sour cream
  3 egg yolks
½ teaspoon salt
    Dash pepper

In a large bowl combine the 1 egg and milk; stir in soft bread crumbs, onion, the 1½ teaspoons salt, and the ⅛ teaspoon pepper. Add beef; mix well. Pat the meat mixture into an 8x8x2-inch baking dish.

Bake at 350° for 25 minutes. Drain off excess fat. Slice the tomatoes atop partially baked meat loaf; sprinkle with a little salt and pepper. Cover with cheese slices.

Beat the egg whites to soft peaks (tips bend over), 1 minute; set aside. In small mixer bowl combine the flour, sour cream, egg yolks, the ½ teaspoon salt, and the dash pepper. Beat till smooth. Fold beaten egg whites into yolk mixture. Pour egg mixture over cheese-covered meat.

Return to oven till golden brown, about 30 minutes. Let stand 5 minutes before cutting. Spoon some of the sauce in bottom of dish over each serving. Makes 8 or 9 servings.

Italian Meat Loaf

2 **eggs**
1 **15-ounce can pizza sauce**
1 **cup finely crushed saltine**
crackers (28 crackers)
½ **cup finely chopped onion**
½ **cup finely chopped green**
pepper
½ **teaspoon garlic salt**
Dash pepper
1½ **pounds ground beef**
1 **4-ounce can chopped mushrooms**
1½ **cups small curd cream-style**
cottage cheese (12 ounces)
1 **tablespoon snipped parsley**
½ **teaspoon dried oregano,**
crushed

In a large bowl, combine *1* of the eggs and ½ *cup* of the pizza sauce. Stir in ½ *cup* of the cracker crumbs, the chopped onion, chopped green pepper, garlic salt, and pepper. Add beef; mix well. Pat ⅓ of the meat mixture into bottom of 8x8x2-inch baking pan.

Drain mushrooms; combine with remaining egg, remaining ½ cup crumbs, cottage cheese, parsley, and oregano. Spread evenly over meat in pan. Top with remaining meat mixture.

Bake at 350° for 50 minutes. Let stand 10 minutes before serving. In small saucepan, heat the remaining pizza sauce; pass with meat loaf. Makes 8 servings.

Twin Meat Loaves

4 **slices bread, cubed**
(3 cups)
¾ **cup milk**
2 **beaten eggs**
¼ **cup finely chopped onion**
¼ **cup finely chopped celery**
1 **tablespoon Worcestershire**
sauce
1½ **teaspoons salt**
½ **teaspoon poultry seasoning**
⅛ **teaspoon pepper**
1½ **pounds ground beef**
½ **pound ground pork**
¼ **cup chili sauce** *or* ¼ **cup**
catsup and 2 tablespoons
corn syrup

In a bowl soak bread cubes in milk. Add eggs; beat with rotary beater. Stir in chopped onion, chopped celery, Worcestershire sauce, salt, poultry seasoning, and pepper. Add beef and pork; mix thoroughly.

Form meat mixture into two loaves. Place in 13x9x2-inch baking pan. Bake, uncovered, at 350° for 1 hour.

For glaze, spread meat loaves with chili sauce or spread with mixture of catsup and corn syrup. Bake 15 minutes longer. Makes 2 meat loaves, 4 or 5 servings each.

Mini Meat Loaves with Dill

¼ **cup fine dry bread crumbs**
½ **cup milk**
2 **tablespoons finely chopped**
green onion with tops
2 **tablespoons snipped parsley**
½ **teaspoon salt**
½ **teaspoon Worcestershire sauce**
Dash pepper
1 **pound ground beef**
1 **4½-ounce can deviled ham**
Dill Sauce

Combine bread crumbs, milk, green onion, parsley, salt, Worcestershire, and pepper. Add ground beef and deviled ham; mix well. Pat meat mixture into two 5x5-inch squares. Cut each in half to form two rectangles. Broil meat about 4 inches from heat for about 5 minutes; turn and broil 5 minutes longer. Serve with Dill Sauce. Makes 4 servings.

Dill Sauce: In saucepan cook 1 tablespoon finely chopped green onion with tops in 1 tablespoon butter *or* margarine till tender. Blend in 4 teaspoons all-purpose flour, ½ teaspoon instant beef bouillon granules, ½ teaspoon dried dillweed, ½ teaspoon paprika, and ¼ teaspoon salt. Add ½ cup milk and ½ cup water all at once. Cook and stir till bubbly. Makes about 1 cup.

Grilling Hamburgers Outdoors

Thickness of Burger	Temperature of Coals	Open Grill		Covered Grill	
		Rare	Medium	Rare	Medium
		(approximate total time in minutes)			
½ inch	Medium-hot	8 to 10	10 to 12	7 to 9	8 to 10
	Medium	10 to 12	12 to 15	8 to 10	10 to 12
¾ inch	Medium-hot	10 to 12	12 to 15	8 to 10	10 to 12
	Medium	12 to 15	14 to 18	10 to 12	12 to 15

Shape meat mixture into patties as nearly equal in diameter and thickness as possible. To estimate temperature of coals, hold hand, palm side down, about *4 inches* above coals. Count seconds "one thousand one, one thousand two," and so on. When you can hold your hand comfortably over the coals for 2 to 3 seconds, they have a temperature of *medium-hot;* 3 to 4 seconds indicates *medium*. Grill the burgers for about half of the given time; turn and continue grilling to desired doneness.

Bull's-eye Burgers

¾ cup soft bread crumbs
   (1 slice)
¼ cup milk
½ teaspoon onion salt
¼ teaspoon garlic salt
   Dash pepper
1 pound ground beef
2 hard-cooked eggs
   Hot-style catsup *or* chili
   sauce

In bowl combine bread crumbs, milk, onion salt, garlic salt, and pepper. Add ground beef; mix well. Shape meat mixture into 4 patties, ¾ inch thick. Cut eggs in half lengthwise. Press one egg half, cut side up, into each meat patty. Place in 8x8x2-inch baking pan. Cover. Bake at 350° for 20 to 25 minutes.

   Meanwhile, in small saucepan heat catsup or chili sauce. Serve with burgers. Makes 4 servings.

Planked Chopped Steak

1½ pounds potatoes
 2 tablespoons butter
 2 beaten eggs
1½ pounds ground beef sirloin
 ½ teaspoon salt
 ⅛ teaspoon pepper
 8 small carrots, cooked and
   buttered
 2 cups peas, cooked and
   buttered
   Snipped parsley

Peel and quarter the potatoes. Cook, covered, in boiling salted water till tender, about 25 minutes. Drain well. Add the butter and eggs to potatoes; beat till fluffy. Add salt and pepper to taste; set aside.

   Shape ground beef into 4 oval patties about 1 inch thick. In skillet cook patties till rare, about 5 minutes per side. Place each on a well-buttered seasoned steak plank; sprinkle with the salt and pepper. Place potatoes in pastry bag; pipe onto plank to form border 1-inch larger than patty.

   Place 2 planks under broiler, 4 inches from heat; broil till potatoes brown lightly, about 4 minutes. Repeat with remaining planks. Arrange carrots and peas within potato border; sprinkle with parsley. Makes 4 servings.

Pepper Burgers with Thyme Sauce

    1 beaten egg
    2 tablespoons milk
  ¾ cup soft bread crumbs
  ¾ teaspoon salt
  ¼ teaspoon ground nutmeg
    1 pound ground beef
    1 medium onion, chopped (½ cup)
    1 cup beef broth
    1 tablespoon all-purpose flour
 1½ teaspoons Worcestershire sauce
  ½ teaspoon dried thyme, crushed
    1 medium green pepper

In bowl combine egg and milk; stir in bread crumbs, salt, and nutmeg. Add ground beef; mix well. Shape into four patties. In a 10-inch skillet, cook patties over medium heat for 3 to 4 minutes. Turn and cook almost to desired doneness, 3 to 4 minutes more. Remove from skillet.

Cook onion in skillet drippings till tender but not brown. Drain off excess fat. Blend beef broth and flour; stir into skillet along with Worcestershire and thyme. Cook and stir till thickened and bubbly. Return burgers to skillet.

Cut green pepper in strips; add to skillet. Simmer, covered, till burgers are heated through, 2 to 3 minutes. Serve with hot cooked rice, if desired. Makes 4 servings.

Sauerbraten Burgers

  ½ cup crushed gingersnaps
       (8 cookies)
    1 8-ounce can tomato sauce
  ¼ cup finely chopped onion
  ¼ cup raisins (optional)
  ½ teaspoon salt
    1 pound ground beef
    2 tablespoons brown sugar
    2 tablespoons vinegar
    2 tablespoons water
    1 teaspoon prepared mustard
       Dash pepper
       Hot cooked noodles or rice

Reserve 2 *tablespoons* of the crushed gingersnaps. Mix remaining gingersnaps with 2 *tablespoons* of the tomato sauce, onion, raisins, and salt. Add meat; mix well. Form four 4-inch patties; brown in skillet. Drain off fat. Blend remaining tomato sauce, brown sugar, vinegar, water, mustard, and pepper. Pour over burgers. Cover; simmer 10 to 15 minutes, spooning sauce over meat. Remove burgers; keep warm.

Stir reserved gingersnaps into sauce in skillet. Cook and stir till bubbly. Pour some sauce over burgers; pass remaining. Serve with noodles. Makes 4 servings.

Microwave cooking directions: Prepare patties as above. Place in 8x8x2-inch glass baking dish. Cook, covered, in countertop microwave oven 3 minutes. Give dish a half turn; micro-cook 2 minutes more. Drain off excess fat. Blend remaining tomato sauce, reserved gingersnaps, brown sugar, vinegar, water, mustard, and pepper; pour over meat. Micro-cook, covered, 2 minutes. Stir sauce and turn dish; micro-cook, covered, 2 minutes more.

Bean and Rice Burgers

    1 11½-ounce can condensed bean
       with bacon soup
    1 beaten egg
  ¼ cup regular rice
  ¼ cup wheat germ
    1 tablespoon instant minced onion
  ¾ teaspoon garlic salt
  ¼ teaspoon seasoned pepper
  ¼ teaspoon chili powder
    1 pound ground beef
    1 16-ounce can barbecue beans
  ½ cup shredded sharp American
       cheese (2 ounces)

Blend together soup and ⅔ cup water. Combine ½ *cup* of the soup mixture with the egg; stir in uncooked rice, wheat germ, onion, garlic salt, seasoned pepper, and chili powder. Add meat; mix well. Shape into six patties.

In skillet, brown patties on both sides; drain off excess fat. Combine the remaining soup mixture, beans, and ½ cup water; spoon around patties. Cover and simmer 55 minutes, stirring carefully once or twice.

Uncover; sprinkle the meat patties with shredded cheese. Continue cooking till cheese melts, 1 to 2 minutes more. Makes 6 servings.

Check the index for recipe pages of these favorites: *Spicy Meatball Sandwiches, Biscuit-Meatball Pie, Chili Meatball Supper, Meatballs Oriental-Style,* and *German Meatballs with Spaetzle.*

German Meatballs with Spaetzle

  1 **beaten egg**
¼ **cup milk**
¼ **cup fine dry bread crumbs**
  1 **tablespoon snipped parsley**
¼ **teaspoon poultry seasoning**
  1 **pound ground beef**
  1 **10½-ounce can condensed beef broth**
  1 **4-ounce can chopped mushrooms, drained**
½ **cup chopped onion**
  1 **cup dairy sour cream**
  1 **tablespoon all-purpose flour**
½ **to 1 teaspoon caraway seed**
    Spaetzle

Combine egg and milk; stir in crumbs, parsley, poultry seasoning, ½ teaspoon salt, and dash pepper. Add meat; mix well. Shape in twenty-four 1½-inch meatballs. In skillet, brown meatballs; drain fat. Add broth, mushrooms, and onion. Cover; simmer 30 minutes.

Blend sour cream, flour, and caraway seed; stir into meatballs and sauce in skillet. Cook and stir till thickened. Serve with Spaetzle. Sprinkle with snipped parsley, if desired. Makes 4 to 6 servings.

Spaetzle: Mix 2 cups all-purpose flour and 1 teaspoon salt. Add 2 beaten eggs and 1 cup milk; beat well. Let rest 5 to 10 minutes. Place batter in coarse-sieved colander (like basket for deep-fat fryer). Hold over large kettle of rapidly boiling salted water. Press batter through colander with rubber spatula. Cook and stir 5 minutes; drain.

Oven-Baked Meatballs

3 beaten eggs
½ cup milk
3 cups soft bread crumbs
   (4 slices)
½ cup finely chopped onion
2 teaspoons salt
3 pounds ground beef

In a bowl combine eggs and milk; stir in crumbs, onion, and salt. Add meat; mix well. Chill. With wet hands shape meat into 72 one-inch balls. Place in two 15½x10½x1-inch baking pans. Bake at 375° for 25 to 30 minutes. Place meatballs on another baking pan to cool; place in freezer just till frozen. Using 24 meatballs per package, wrap in moisture-vapor-proof bags. Seal, label, and freeze. Makes 72 meatballs.

Microwave cooking directions: Prepare meat mixture and shape as above. Arrange *unbaked* meatballs on baking pans; place in freezer just till frozen. Using 24 meatballs per package, wrap in moisture-vaporproof bags. Seal, label, and freeze. To use, place meatballs in single layer in 12x7½x2-inch glass baking dish. In countertop microwave oven cook, covered, till thawed, about 4 minutes; rearrange meatballs after each minute. Micro-cook, covered, till done, about 6 minutes; turn meatballs over and rearrange twice. Drain.

Quick Spaghetti and Meatballs

2 16-ounce cans tomatoes, cut up
1 6-ounce can tomato paste
½ cup dry red wine
½ cup chopped onion
½ cup chopped green pepper
1 clove garlic, minced
2 teaspoons sugar
1 teaspoon salt
1 teaspoon dried oregano,
   crushed
½ teaspoon chili powder
24 frozen Oven-Baked Meatballs
   (see above)
   Hot cooked spaghetti
   Grated Parmesan cheese

In Dutch oven combine the undrained tomatoes, tomato paste, wine, onion, green pepper, garlic, sugar, salt, oregano, chili powder. Stir in ¾ cup water and bring to boiling.

Stir in frozen cooked meatballs. (If using meatballs from microwave cooking directions, be sure to micro-cook *before* adding to tomato mixture.)

Simmer, uncovered, till heated through and of desired consistency, about 30 minutes. Stir occasionally.

Serve meatballs and tomato sauce over spaghetti; pass the Parmesan cheese. Makes 6 to 8 servings.

Meatballs with Biscuit Topper

1 beaten egg
1 10¾-ounce can condensed
   cream of celery soup
¾ cup soft bread crumbs
   (1 slice)
1 tablespoon onion soup mix
1 pound ground beef
2 tablespoons cooking oil *or*
   shortening
   Biscuit Topper
2 tablespoons all-purpose flour
½ teaspoon paprika
½ cup water
1 3-ounce can chopped
   mushrooms

Blend egg, *2 tablespoons* of the canned soup, bread crumbs, and dry onion soup mix. Add beef; mix well. Shape into 12 meatballs. Brown meatballs over medium heat in hot oil, 8 to 10 minutes. Drain off excess fat. Prepare Biscuit Topper; set aside. Combine remaining canned soup, flour, and paprika. Stir in water and undrained mushrooms. Pour over meatballs in skillet; bring to boiling. Pour boiling mixture into 1½-quart casserole; top immediately with Biscuit Topper. Bake, uncovered, at 400° for 15 minutes. Serves 4.

Biscuit Topper: Combine ½ cup all-purpose flour, 1 teaspoon baking powder, 1 teaspoon dry onion soup mix, and ⅛ teaspoon celery salt. Blend ¼ cup milk and 2 teaspoons cooking oil. Stir into flour mixture just till blended. Combine ¾ cup soft bread crumbs with 2 tablespoons melted butter. Divide dough into 8 portions; drop into buttered crumbs. Turn to coat all sides; place atop bubbling meat mixture.

Meatballs Oriental-Style (pictured on page 47)

1 beaten egg
3 tablespoons milk
¾ cup soft bread crumbs
2 tablespoons finely chopped
    onion
¾ teaspoon salt
    Dash pepper
1 pound ground beef
2 tablespoons shortening
1 5-ounce can water chestnuts
1 cup bias-cut celery
½ cup sliced green onion with
    tops
1 15½-ounce can pineapple chunks
2 tablespoons cornstarch
2 teaspoons instant beef
    bouillon granules
1 cup boiling water
1 tablespoon brown sugar
2 tablespoons soy sauce
1 medium tomato, peeled
1 6-ounce package frozen
    pea pods, thawed
    Chow mein noodles or hot
    cooked rice

Combine egg and milk; stir in bread crumbs, chopped onion, salt, and pepper. Add ground beef; mix well. Shape into 24 one-inch balls. In skillet, brown meatballs in hot shortening; drain off excess fat. Drain and slice the water chestnuts; add to skillet with celery and green onion. Cook till celery and onion are crisp-tender, about 5 minutes.

Drain pineapple, reserving syrup; add water to reserved syrup to make 1 cup liquid. Blend cornstarch with syrup mixture. Dissolve bouillon in the 1 cup boiling water; combine with cornstarch mixture, brown sugar, and soy sauce. Add to meat mixture. Cook and stir till mixture is thickened and bubbly.

Cut tomato in eighths; add to skillet with pineapple and pea pods; heat through. Serve over noodles or rice. Makes 4 or 5 servings.

Porcupine Meatballs

1 beaten egg
1 10¾-ounce can condensed
    tomato soup
¼ cup regular rice
2 tablespoons finely chopped
    onion
1 tablespoon snipped parsley
½ teaspoon salt
⅛ teaspoon pepper
1 pound ground beef
½ cup water
1 teaspoon Worcestershire sauce

In bowl combine egg and ¼ *cup* of the tomato soup. Stir in the uncooked rice, chopped onion, parsley, salt, and pepper. Add ground beef and mix well. Shape meat mixture in 20 small balls; place in 10-inch skillet.

Mix remaining soup with water and Worcestershire; pour over meatballs. Bring to boiling; reduce heat. Cover and simmer 35 to 40 minutes; stir often. Makes 4 or 5 servings.

Shaping Ground Beef Mixtures

A light touch is the secret to better burgers, meatballs, and meat loaves. Too much handling gives them a compact texture, so mix carefully. When shaping burgers or meatballs, try to keep them uniform in size. Use a ⅓- or ½-cup measure for each burger. A ¼-cup measure *or* 1 or 2 tablespoons can be used for meatballs. Another shaping trick for burgers is to form the meat into a roll 3 inches in diameter and cut in ½-inch-thick slices. For meatballs, cut a 1-inch diameter roll in 1-inch slices, or pat meat to a 1-inch-thick square and cut in 1-inch cubes.

Cherry Tomato Meatballs

1 beaten egg
½ cup milk
¾ cup soft bread crumbs (1 slice)
¼ cup finely chopped onion
1 teaspoon Worcestershire sauce
¾ teaspoon salt
½ teaspoon dried oregano, crushed
⅛ teaspoon pepper
1 pound ground beef
12 cherry tomatoes

In mixing bowl combine the egg and milk; stir in bread crumbs, onion, Worcestershire sauce, salt, oregano, and pepper. Add meat; mix well. Shape about ¼ cup of the meat mixture evenly around each cherry tomato to form round meatballs. Place in 13x9x2-inch baking pan. Bake at 375° for 25 to 30 minutes. Makes 4 servings.

Microwave cooking directions: Prepare meatballs as above. Place in single layer in 12x7½x2-inch glass baking dish. Cook, covered, in countertop microwave oven about 8 minutes; turn and rearrange meatballs twice. Drain off fat.

Meatball Carbonade

3 slices bacon
1 12-ounce can beer (1½ cups)
1 beaten egg
¼ cup fine dry bread crumbs
¾ teaspoon salt
1 pound ground beef
2 medium onions, thinly sliced
3 tablespoons all-purpose flour
1 teaspoon instant beef bouillon granules
1 teaspoon brown sugar
1 teaspoon vinegar
½ teaspoon salt
¼ teaspoon dried thyme, crushed
2 tablespoons snipped parsley

In medium skillet cook bacon till crisp; crumble and set aside, reserving drippings. In bowl combine ¼ *cup* of the beer, egg, bread crumbs, the ¾ teaspoon salt, and dash pepper; add ground beef and mix well. Shape meat mixture into 24 meatballs. Brown on all sides in bacon drippings. Transfer meatballs to 1½-quart casserole.

In same skillet cook onions till golden; stir in flour. Add remaining beer, bouillon granules, brown sugar, vinegar, the ½ teaspoon salt, thyme, and dash pepper. Cook and stir till thickened and bubbly. Pour over meatballs.

Cover and bake at 350° for 45 minutes. Top with parsley and crumbled bacon just before serving. Makes 4 servings.

Swedish Meatballs

½ cup chopped onion
3 tablespoons butter
1 beaten egg
1 cup light cream
1½ cups soft bread crumbs
¼ cup finely snipped parsley
1¼ teaspoons salt
    Dash pepper
    Dash ground nutmeg
    Dash ground ginger
1½ pounds ground beef *or* ¾ pound ground beef, ½ pound ground veal, and ¼ pound ground pork
2 tablespoons all-purpose flour
1 teaspoon instant beef bouillon granules
½ teaspoon instant coffee crystals

Cook onion in *1 tablespoon* of the butter till tender. In mixing bowl, combine egg and cream; stir in bread crumbs, cooked onion, parsley, salt, pepper, nutmeg, and ginger. Add meats. Mix well by hand or on medium speed of electric mixer. Shape into ¾- to 1-inch balls (mixture will be soft; for easier shaping, wet hands or chill mixture first).

Brown meatballs half at a time in the remaining 2 tablespoons butter; remove from skillet. Stir flour, bouillon granules, and coffee crystals into pan juices; add 1¼ cups water. Cook and stir till thickened and bubbly. Add meatballs. Cover; simmer about 30 minutes, basting meatballs occasionally. Makes about 60 appetizer meatballs.

When a soup is the whole meal, make sure it's a hearty one like *Mini-Meatball Mine-strone* (see recipe, page 59). A variety of vegetables plus meatballs and pasta give it a high rating.

One-Dish Meals

Manicotti

8 manicotti shells
1 pound ground beef
2 6-ounce cans tomato paste
½ cup chopped onion
⅓ cup snipped parsley
1 tablespoon dried basil, crushed
1½ teaspoons salt
1 large clove garlic, minced
2 cups water
2 beaten eggs
3 cups ricotta *or* cream-style cottage cheese, drained (24 ounces)
¾ cup grated Romano *or* Parmesan cheese
¼ teaspoon salt

Cook manicotti shells in boiling salted water till just tender, 15 to 20 minutes; drain. Rinse shells in cold water.

Meanwhile, in a 3-quart saucepan brown meat lightly. Drain off excess fat. Stir in tomato paste, onion, *half* of the parsley, the basil, the 1½ teaspoons salt, garlic, and dash pepper. Add the 2 cups water; mix well. Simmer, uncovered, for 15 minutes, stirring occasionally.

In bowl combine eggs, ricotta or cottage cheese, ½ *cup* of the Romano or Parmesan cheese, remaining parsley, the ¼ teaspoon salt, and dash pepper. Stuff cooked manicotti shells with cheese mixture, using a small spoon (or slit shells lengthwise with scissors and open to fill).

Pour *half* of the tomato-meat sauce into a 12x7½x2-inch baking dish. Arrange stuffed manicotti in dish; top with remaining sauce. Sprinkle with the remaining ¼ cup Romano cheese. Bake, uncovered, at 350° for 40 to 45 minutes. Let stand 10 minutes before serving. Makes 6 to 8 servings.

Texas Beef Skillet

1 pound ground beef
¾ cup chopped onion
1½ teaspoons chili powder
½ teaspoon salt
½ teaspoon garlic salt
1 16-ounce can tomatoes, cut up
1 15½-ounce can red kidney beans
¾ cup quick-cooking rice
¾ cup water
3 tablespoons chopped green pepper
¾ cup shredded sharp American cheese (3 ounces)

In skillet cook ground beef and onion till beef is brown and onion is tender; drain off fat.

Sprinkle meat mixture with chili powder, salt, and garlic salt. Stir in undrained tomatoes, undrained beans, uncooked rice, water, and green pepper.

Cover and simmer, stirring occasionally, for 20 minutes. Top with cheese. Cover and heat till cheese melts, about 3 minutes longer. Sprinkle with crushed corn chips, if desired. Makes 6 servings.

Dinner in a Pepper

8 large green peppers
1 pound ground beef
½ cup chopped onion
3 medium tomatoes, peeled and chopped
1 8-ounce can whole kernel corn, drained
1 8-ounce can cream-style corn
1 teaspoon salt
¾ teaspoon dried basil, crushed
   Dash pepper
¾ cup soft bread crumbs (1 slice)
1 tablespoon butter, melted

Cut tops from green peppers; discard seeds and membranes. Chop enough of the tops to make ¼ cup; set aside. Cook the whole green peppers in boiling water for 5 minutes; drain well. Sprinkle insides of peppers lightly with salt.

In skillet cook ground beef, onion, and the ¼ cup chopped green pepper till meat is brown and onion is tender. Add tomatoes; simmer till tomatoes are cooked, about 4 minutes. Drain off liquid. Add whole kernel corn, cream-style corn, salt, basil, and pepper to skillet; mix well.

Stuff peppers with the meat mixture. Toss crumbs with melted butter to combine; sprinkle atop peppers. Place the stuffed peppers in a 13x9x2-inch baking dish. Bake, uncovered, at 350° for 35 to 40 minutes. Makes 8 servings.

Looking for new menu ideas? Plan an Italian-style dinner featuring *Manicotti.* The large pasta tubes are filled with a creamy cheese mixture and baked in a beef-tomato sauce.

Skillet Hamburger Pie

1½ pounds ground beef
½ cup chopped celery
½ cup chopped onion
1 15½-ounce can cut green beans,
    drained
1 10¾-ounce can condensed
    golden mushroom soup
1 teaspoon Worcestershire sauce
2 cups instant mashed potato
    buds
½ cup dairy sour cream
1 tablespoon snipped chives
    or parsley (optional)
    Paprika
⅓ cup shredded American cheese

In skillet cook beef, celery, and onion till meat is brown and onion is tender. Drain off fat. Stir in drained beans, mushroom soup, Worcestershire sauce, ¼ cup water, ¼ teaspoon salt, and ⅛ teaspoon pepper. Simmer to blend flavors, about 10 minutes, stirring occasionally.

Meanwhile, whip dry potato buds and 2 cups boiling water; stir in sour cream, snipped chives, and ½ teaspoon salt. Spoon potatoes in mounds over meat mixture. Sprinkle with paprika; top with shredded cheese. Cover and heat till cheese melts. Makes 6 servings.

Individual Beefburger Stack-Ups

2 beaten eggs
¼ cup milk
1 teaspoon salt
1 teaspoon Worcestershire sauce
    Dash pepper
1½ pounds ground beef
    Packaged instant mashed
    potatoes (enough for
    4 servings)
½ cup dairy sour cream
¼ cup chopped green onion
    with tops
2 tablespoons chopped pimiento
¼ teaspoon salt
3 slices sharp American cheese

In a bowl combine eggs, milk, the 1 teaspoon salt, Worcestershire sauce, and pepper. Add ground beef; mix well. Form mixture into 12 patties. Place one beef patty in *each* of 6 individual casserole dishes.

Stir dry instant potatoes into 1 cup boiling water. Stir in sour cream, green onion, chopped pimiento, and the ¼ teaspoon salt; spoon over meat patties. Top each casserole with one of the remaining meat patties.

Bake, uncovered, at 375° for 45 minutes. Cut cheese slices in half; arrange atop casseroles. Bake till cheese melts, about 2 minutes longer. If desired, heat catsup and pass to spoon atop casseroles. Makes 6 servings.

Layered Hamburger Bake

1 10-ounce package frozen
    chopped spinach
4 ounces medium noodles (3 cups)
1 pound ground beef
1 15-ounce can tomato sauce
1 teaspoon sugar
½ teaspoon salt
¼ teaspoon garlic salt
⅛ teaspoon pepper
1 8-ounce package cream cheese,
    softened
½ cup dairy sour cream
3 tablespoons milk
2 tablespoons finely chopped
    onion
½ cup shredded Cheddar cheese
    (2 ounces)

Cook frozen spinach according to package directions; drain well. Cook noodles in a large amount of boiling salted water till tender, about 10 minutes; drain well.

In skillet, brown ground beef; drain off fat. Stir in tomato sauce, sugar, salt, garlic salt, pepper, and the cooked noodles. Stir together the cream cheese, sour cream, milk, and finely chopped onion.

In a 2-quart casserole layer *half* of the ground beef-noodle mixture, *half* of the cream cheese mixture, *all* of the spinach, and then the remaining beef-noodle mixture.

Bake, covered, at 350° till bubbly, about 40 minutes. Uncover; spread with remaining cream cheese mixture. Sprinkle with the Cheddar cheese. Bake, uncovered, till cheese melts, about 10 minutes longer. Makes 6 servings.

Biscuit-Meatball Pie (pictured on page 47)

1 beaten egg
1 cup soft bread crumbs
2 tablespoons snipped parsley
¾ teaspoon salt
    Dash pepper
1 pound ground beef
½ cup chopped onion
2 tablespoons cooking oil
1 10¾-ounce can condensed
    cream of mushroom soup
1 soup can milk (1¼ cups)
1 10-ounce package frozen
    mixed vegetables
¼ teaspoon pepper
1½ cups packaged biscuit mix
½ cup shredded sharp American
    cheese (2 ounces)

Combine beaten egg and ¼ cup water. Stir in bread crumbs, parsley, salt, and the dash pepper. Add ground beef; mix well. Shape mixture into twenty-four 1-inch balls. In skillet cook meatballs and onion in hot oil till meatballs are brown; drain off excess fat.

Stir in soup, milk, vegetables, and the ¼ teaspoon pepper. Heat mixture to boiling; reduce heat and simmer, covered, for 20 minutes, stirring occasionally.

Meanwhile, in bowl combine biscuit mix, shredded cheese, and ⅓ cup water; stir till dough clings to spoon. Turn out onto surface dusted with additional biscuit mix; knead 5 or 6 times. Roll out to a 7-inch circle. Cut in 6 wedges.

Turn hot meatball mixture into a 2-quart casserole. Top with biscuit wedges. Bake, uncovered, at 425° till biscuits are done, about 15 minutes. Makes 6 servings.

Chili Meatball Supper (pictured on page 47)

3 large onions, chopped (3 cups)
3 large green peppers, chopped
3 15½-ounce cans red kidney
    beans, drained
3 16-ounce cans tomatoes, cut up
2 12-ounce cans whole kernel
    corn
1 15-ounce can tomato sauce
2 tablespoons chili powder
3 bay leaves
72 frozen Oven-Baked Meatballs
    (see recipe, page 48)
1½ cups shredded Cheddar cheese
1½ cups crushed corn chips

In a 6-quart Dutch oven combine the onion, green pepper, drained beans, undrained tomatoes, undrained corn, tomato sauce, chili powder, bay leaves, and 1 tablespoon salt.

Bring to boiling; stir in frozen meatballs. (If using meatballs from microwave cooking directions, be sure to micro-cook *before* adding to mixture.)

Cover and simmer till meatballs are heated through, about 45 minutes, stirring occasionally. Remove the bay leaves. Pass shredded cheese and corn chips to sprinkle atop each serving. Makes 18 to 20 servings.

Beef-Filled Corn Bread Squares (pictured on page 40)

1 pound ground beef
⅓ cup chopped onion
1 clove garlic, minced
¼ cup catsup
¾ teaspoon salt
1 10-ounce package corn bread
    mix
½ cup shredded American cheese
2 tablespoons cold water
2 teaspoons cornstarch
1 8-ounce can tomatoes, cut up
2 tablespoons chopped seeded
    canned green chili peppers
2 tablespoons chopped green
    pepper
1 teaspoon Worcestershire sauce

In skillet cook beef, onion, and garlic till meat is brown; drain off fat. Stir in catsup and salt; set aside.

In bowl prepare corn bread mix according to package directions. Spread *half* of the batter in a greased 8x8x2-inch baking pan. Spoon beef mixture over batter in pan; sprinkle with cheese. Spread remaining batter over cheese.

Bake, uncovered, at 350° till corn bread is done, 30 to 35 minutes. Let stand 5 minutes before cutting.

Meanwhile, in small saucepan blend cold water with cornstarch. Stir in the undrained tomatoes, chili peppers, green pepper, and Worcestershire sauce. Cook and stir till thickened and bubbly. Cut corn bread in squares; serve sauce over. Makes 6 servings.

Cheeseburger Pie

1 pound ground beef
½ cup chopped onion
1 8-ounce can tomato sauce
1 4-ounce can chopped
   mushrooms, drained
¼ cup snipped parsley
¼ teaspoon salt
¼ teaspoon dried oregano,
   crushed
⅛ teaspoon pepper
2 packages refrigerated crescent
   rolls (8 rolls each)
3 eggs
6 slices sharp American cheese
   (6 ounces)
1 tablespoon water

In skillet cook ground beef and onion till meat is brown and onion is tender; drain off fat. Stir in tomato sauce, drained mushrooms, parsley, salt, oregano, and pepper.

Unroll *one* package of the crescent rolls and separate into triangles. Place in a lightly greased 9-inch pie plate, pressing edges together to form a pie shell.

Separate *one* of the eggs; set yolk aside. Beat egg white with the remaining 2 eggs. Pour *half* the beaten egg over pie shell. Spoon meat mixture into shell. Arrange the cheese slices atop; spread with remaining beaten egg.

Mix reserved egg yolk with water; lightly brush some over edge of pastry. Reserve remaining yolk mixture.

Unroll second package of crescent rolls. Place the four sections of dough together to form a 12x6-inch rectangle. Seal edges and perforations together. Roll out dough to a 12-inch square. Place dough atop filling. Trim; seal and flute edges. Cut slits in top crust for escape of steam. Brush top with the remaining egg yolk mixture.

Loosely cover edge with a strip of foil to prevent over-browning. Bake at 350° for 20 minutes. Cover center of pie loosely with foil. Bake 20 minutes longer. Let stand 10 minutes before serving. Makes 6 servings.

Skillet Enchiladas

1 10¾-ounce can condensed
   cream of mushroom soup
1 10-ounce can enchilada sauce
¼ cup milk
2 tablespoons chopped seeded
   canned green chili peppers
8 canned *or* frozen tortillas
   Cooking oil (optional)
2½ cups shredded sharp American
   cheese (10 ounces)
½ cup chopped pitted ripe
   olives
1 pound ground beef
½ cup chopped onion

In a saucepan combine cream of mushroom soup, enchilada sauce, milk, and green chili peppers; heat till bubbly.

Thaw frozen tortillas. Dip tortillas, one at a time, in the hot sauce just till tortillas become limp. (Or, heat some cooking oil in a small skillet; dip tortillas in till limp.) Drain tortillas. Set aside ½ cup cheese. Place ¼ cup cheese on *each* tortilla; sprinkle with olives. Roll up as for jelly roll.

In skillet cook beef and onion till meat is brown and onion is tender; drain off fat. Stir in hot sauce mixture. Arrange tortillas seam side down in sauce in the skillet. Bring to boiling; reduce heat. Cover and cook till heated through, about 5 minutes. Sprinkle with the remaining ½ cup cheese; cover and cook till cheese melts, about 1 minute longer. Makes 6 to 8 servings.

Microwave cooking directions: In a 12x7½x2-inch glass baking dish combine mushroom soup, enchilada sauce, milk, and green chili peppers. Cook in a countertop micro-wave oven till bubbly, about 5 minutes, stirring 3 times.

Dip tortillas in hot sauce or cooking oil as directed above. Fill and roll up as directed above.

In glass bowl crumble beef; add onion. Micro-cook, covered, till meat is done, about 5 minutes, stirring several times. Drain off fat. Stir meat into sauce in baking dish.

Arrange tortillas seam side down in sauce. Micro-cook, uncovered, till hot, about 8 minutes. Give dish ¼ turn every 3 minutes. Sprinkle with remaining ½ cup cheese.

Cheeseburger Pie is a lot simpler to make than it looks. Prepare the crust of this luscious pie with refrigerated crescent rolls, then brush with egg yolk for a rich golden color.

Olive Spaghetti Sauce

1 pound ground beef
½ pound bulk Italian sausage
1 28-ounce can tomatoes, cut up
2 6-ounce cans tomato paste
1½ cups Burgundy
1 cup water
1 cup chopped onion
¾ cup chopped green pepper
1½ teaspoons Worcestershire
    sauce
1 teaspoon sugar
1 teaspoon salt
½ teaspoon chili powder
⅛ teaspoon pepper
3 bay leaves
2 cloves garlic, minced
1 6-ounce can sliced mushrooms
½ cup sliced pimiento-stuffed
    green olives
20 ounces spaghetti
    Grated Parmesan cheese

In large Dutch oven brown beef and sausage; drain off fat. Stir in undrained tomatoes, tomato paste, Burgundy, water, onion, green pepper, Worcestershire, sugar, salt, chili powder, pepper, bay leaves, and garlic. Simmer, uncovered, for 2 hours; stir occasionally. Remove bay leaves. Stir in mushrooms and olives; simmer 30 minutes longer.

Cook spaghetti according to package directions; drain. Serve with sauce; pass Parmesan. Makes 8 to 10 servings.

Crockery cooker directions: Use above ingredients *except* decrease Burgundy to ½ cup, decrease water to ⅓ cup, and add 2 tablespoons cornstarch as directed.

In skillet, brown meats; drain. Spoon meat into electric slow crockery cooker. Add undrained tomatoes, tomato paste, ½ cup Burgundy, ⅓ cup water, onion, green pepper, Worcestershire, sugar, salt, chili powder, pepper, bay leaves, garlic, mushrooms, and olives. Cover; cook on low-heat setting for 10 to 12 hours.

Turn cooker to high-heat setting; heat, covered, till bubbly, about 10 minutes. Blend 2 tablespoons cornstarch with 2 tablespoons cold water; stir into sauce. Cover; cook 10 minutes longer. Remove bay leaves. Serve as above.

Cheeseburger Chowder

1 pound ground beef
2 medium potatoes, peeled and
    cubed (2 cups)
½ cup chopped celery
¼ cup chopped onion
2 tablespoons chopped green
    pepper
1 tablespoon instant beef
    bouillon granules
½ teaspoon salt
2½ cups milk
3 tablespoons all-purpose flour
1 cup shredded sharp Cheddar
    cheese (4 ounces)

In 3-quart saucepan brown beef. Drain off excess fat. Stir in potatoes, celery, onion, green pepper, bouillon granules, salt, and 1½ cups water. Cover and cook till vegetables are tender, 15 to 20 minutes.

Blend ½ *cup* of the milk with the flour. Add to saucepan along with remaining milk. Cook and stir till thickened and bubbly. Add cheese; heat and stir just till cheese melts. Garnish with additional shredded cheese, if desired. Makes 6 to 8 servings.

Sausage and Beef Chili

1½ pounds ground beef
½ pound bulk pork sausage
1 cup chopped onion
2 15½-ounce cans red kidney
    beans, drained
1 28-ounce can tomatoes, cut up
1 cup chopped green pepper
1 cup thinly sliced celery
1 6-ounce can tomato paste
2 cloves garlic, minced
2 teaspoons salt
2 teaspoons chili powder

In Dutch oven cook beef, sausage, and onion till meats are brown; drain off excess fat. Stir in beans, undrained tomatoes, green pepper, celery, tomato paste, garlic, salt, and chili powder. Cover; simmer 1 to 1½ hours, stirring occasionally. Makes 10 to 12 servings.

Note: If a less thick chili is desired, substitute one 8-ounce can tomato sauce for the tomato paste and do not drain the kidney beans.

Crockery cooker directions: Use above ingredients. Cook meats and onion till meat is brown; drain. Spoon meat into electric slow crockery cooker. Add remaining ingredients. Cover; cook on low-heat setting for 8 to 10 hours.

Sour Cream Chili

1 pound ground beef
2 11¼-ounce cans condensed
    chili beef soup
2 cups water
2 tablespoons onion soup mix
1 to 1½ teaspoons chili powder
1 cup dairy sour cream
    Shredded cheese
    Chopped onion

In a large saucepan brown the ground beef; drain off excess fat. Stir in the chili beef soup, water, dry onion soup mix, and chili powder. Bring to boiling; cover and simmer for 5 minutes.

Stir some of the hot mixture into the sour cream; return all to saucepan. Heat and stir about 5 minutes longer but *do not boil*. Garnish with shredded cheese and chopped onion. Makes 6 servings

Mini-Meatball Minestrone (pictured on page 51)

1 28-ounce can tomatoes, cut up
2 cups shredded cabbage
2 small zucchini, sliced (2 cups)
1 12-ounce can whole kernel corn
2 ribs celery, sliced (1 cup)
1 medium onion, chopped (½ cup)
½ cup broken vermicelli
    (2 ounces)
½ cup dry red wine
2 tablespoons snipped parsley
1¼ teaspoons instant beef
    bouillon granules
1 teaspoon dried oregano,
    crushed
¼ teaspoon dried basil, crushed
⅛ teaspoon garlic powder
1 beaten egg
¼ cup milk
⅓ cup fine dry bread crumbs
1 teaspoon Worcestershire sauce
1 pound ground beef
    Grated Parmesan cheese

In Dutch oven combine undrained tomatoes, cabbage, zucchini, undrained corn, celery, onion, uncooked vermicelli, red wine, parsley, instant beef bouillon granules, oregano, basil, garlic powder, 4 cups water, ¾ teaspoon salt, and ⅛ teaspoon pepper. Bring mixture to boiling; reduce heat and simmer, covered, for 15 minutes.

Meanwhile, in a bowl combine the egg, milk, bread crumbs, Worcestershire sauce, ½ teaspoon salt, and dash pepper. Add ground beef; mix well. Shape into 36 tiny balls.

In a skillet brown the meatballs, shaking the pan often to keep balls rounded. Drain off excess fat.

Add meatballs to soup. Cover and cook till vegetables and vermicelli are tender, about 15 minutes longer. Pass Parmesan to sprinkle atop. Makes 8 servings.

Taco Salad (pictured on cover)

1 pound ground beef
½ envelope onion soup mix
    (¼ cup)
    Few dashes bottled hot pepper
    sauce
1 small head lettuce, torn in
    bite-size pieces (4 cups)
1 cup shredded sharp Cheddar
    cheese (4 ounces)
1 large tomato, cut in wedges
½ cup sliced pitted ripe olives
¼ cup chopped green pepper *or*
    chopped seeded canned green
    chili peppers
2 cups corn chips
    Taco sauce (optional)

In medium skillet brown beef. Drain off excess fat. Sprinkle dry onion soup mix over meat; stir in ¾ cup water. Simmer mixture, uncovered, till water cooks away, about 10 minutes. Stir in hot pepper sauce.

Meanwhile, in salad bowl combine lettuce, cheese, tomato, olives, and green pepper; toss well. Divide lettuce mixture onto individual salad plates, if desired. Spoon meat mixture over lettuce; garnish with corn chips. Pass taco sauce. Makes 4 to 6 servings.

Pizza and Sandwiches

Pan Pizza

1 13¾-ounce package hot roll mix
1 cup grated Parmesan cheese
½ pound ground beef
¼ cup chopped onion
¼ cup chopped green pepper
1 clove garlic, minced
1 16-ounce can tomatoes, cut up
⅓ cup tomato paste (half of
    a 6-ounce can)
1 4-ounce can mushroom stems
    and pieces, drained
1 teaspoon sugar
1 teaspoon dried basil, crushed
1 teaspoon dried oregano,
    crushed
½ teaspoon fennel seed (optional)
2 cups shredded mozzarella
    cheese (8 ounces)

In large bowl dissolve yeast from roll mix in 1 cup warm water. Stir in flour mixture from mix and ½ *cup* of the Parmesan cheese. Cover and let rest 10 minutes. With greased fingers pat dough out onto bottom and halfway up sides of a greased 15½x10½x1-inch baking pan. Bake at 375° till deep golden brown, 20 to 25 minutes.

Meanwhile, in medium skillet cook ground beef, onion, green pepper, and garlic till meat is brown and onion is tender. Drain off excess fat. Stir in undrained tomatoes, tomato paste, mushrooms, sugar, basil, oregano, fennel, 1 teaspoon salt, and ⅛ teaspoon pepper.

Spread meat mixture over the hot, baked crust. Sprinkle with mozzarella cheese and the remaining Parmesan cheese. Bake at 375° till bubbly, 20 to 25 minutes. Let stand 5 minutes before cutting. Makes 10 servings.

Tostada Pizza (pictured on page 4)

2 tablespoons yellow cornmeal
2 cups packaged biscuit mix
1 pound ground beef
3 tablespoons chopped seeded
    canned green chili peppers
1 1¼-ounce envelope taco
    seasoning mix
1 16-ounce can refried beans
1 cup shredded sharp American
    cheese (4 ounces)
1 cup shredded lettuce
1 tomato, chopped (1 cup)
½ cup chopped onion
    Taco sauce (optional)

Sprinkle a well-greased 12-inch pizza pan with cornmeal. Combine biscuit mix and ½ cup water. Stir with fork till dough follows fork around bowl. Turn dough out on lightly floured surface; knead 5 or 6 times. Roll to 14-inch circle; pat into prepared pizza pan, crimping edges. Bake at 425° till golden brown, about 12 minutes.

Meanwhile, in skillet brown meat; drain. Stir in chili peppers, taco seasoning mix, and ¾ cup water; bring to boiling. Reduce heat; simmer, uncovered, 10 to 15 minutes.

Spread refried beans over crust; top with meat mixture. Bake at 425° for 8 to 10 minutes. Top with cheese; bake 2 minutes more. Garnish with fresh chili peppers, if desired. Pass lettuce, tomato, and onion to sprinkle atop. Dash with taco sauce, if desired. Makes 6 servings.

Stroganoff Sandwich

1 pound ground beef
¼ cup chopped green onion
    with tops
1 cup dairy sour cream
1 teaspoon Worcestershire sauce
⅛ teaspoon garlic powder
1 loaf French bread, unsliced
    Butter *or* margarine, softened
2 tomatoes, sliced
1 green pepper, cut in rings
1 cup shredded American cheese

In skillet cook beef and onion till meat is brown; drain off fat. Stir in sour cream, Worcestershire, garlic powder, and ¾ teaspoon salt; heat through but *do not boil.*

Meanwhile, cut loaf in half lengthwise. Place cut side up on baking sheet. Broil 4 to 5 inches from heat till toasted, 2 to 3 minutes; spread lightly with butter. Spread half the hot meat mixture on each loaf half. Arrange tomato slices alternately with green pepper rings atop meat. Place on baking sheet; broil 3 minutes. Sprinkle with cheese; broil 2 minutes longer. Makes 8 servings.

No one will go hungry when you serve *Pan Pizza*, a homemade adaptation of the pizzeria's thick-crust version. Fennel in the meat mixture gives the beef an Italian sausage flavor.

Spicy Meatball Sandwiches (pictured on page 47)

2 cloves garlic, minced
2 tablespoons butter
1 cup catsup
⅔ cup chili sauce
¼ cup packed brown sugar
2 tablespoons Worcestershire
   sauce
2 tablespoons prepared mustard
2 teaspoons celery seed
½ teaspoon salt
¼ teaspoon bottled hot pepper
   sauce
6 thin slices lemon (½ lemon)
48 frozen Oven-Baked Meatballs
   (see recipe, page 48)
12 hard rolls or frankfurter buns
2 medium onions

In saucepan cook garlic in butter for 4 to 5 minutes. Stir in catsup, chili sauce, brown sugar, Worcestershire sauce, mustard, celery seed, salt, hot pepper sauce, lemon slices, and ½ cup water. Bring to boiling. Stir in frozen meatballs. (If using meatballs from microwave cooking directions, be sure to micro-cook *before* adding to sauce mixture.)

Cover and cook over medium heat till heated through, about 20 minutes; stir occasionally. Remove lemon slices.

Meanwhile, split rolls; hollow out bottoms and tops, leaving edges about ½ inch thick. Slice onions and separate into rings. Serve hot meatball mixture in rolls; top with onion rings. Makes 12 sandwiches.

Taco Burgers

1 pound ground beef
1 16-ounce can tomatoes, cut up
1 teaspoon chili powder
1 teaspoon Worcestershire sauce
¾ teaspoon garlic salt
½ teaspoon sugar
¼ teaspoon dry mustard
8 hamburger buns, split and
   toasted
2 cups shredded lettuce
1 cup shredded American cheese

In skillet brown ground beef; drain off fat. Stir in undrained tomatoes, chili powder, Worcestershire sauce, garlic salt, sugar, and dry mustard. Bring to boiling; reduce heat. Simmer, uncovered, till thickened, 15 to 20 minutes.

Spoon meat mixture onto toasted buns. Sprinkle each of the burgers with lettuce and cheese. Makes 8 sandwiches.

Beer-Kraut Heroes

1 beaten egg
1 12-ounce can beer (1½ cups)
¼ cup fine dry bread crumbs
1 pound ground beef
2 tablespoons cooking oil
1 cup thinly sliced onion
2 tablespoons snipped parsley
1 teaspoon instant beef
   bouillon granules
⅛ teaspoon dried thyme, crushed
1 small bay leaf
1 16-ounce can sauerkraut
1 tablespoon cornstarch
5 hero rolls, split, toasted,
   and buttered

In a bowl combine egg and ¼ *cup* of the beer; stir in bread crumbs, ¾ teaspoon salt, and dash pepper. Add ground beef; mix well. Shape into 20 meatballs. In a heavy skillet brown the meatballs in hot oil; drain off excess fat. Stir in onion, parsley, beef bouillon granules, thyme, bay leaf, and the remaining 1¼ cups beer. Reduce heat; simmer, covered, 20 minutes.

Remove meatballs from skillet. Cover; keep warm. Drain sauerkraut; rinse if milder flavor is desired. Stir kraut into onion mixture in skillet. Return mixture to boiling.

Blend cornstarch with 2 tablespoons cold water; stir into sauerkraut mixture. Cook and stir till thickened and bubbly. Place sauerkraut mixture on rolls; top with warm meatballs. Makes 5 sandwiches.

Who can resist *Taco Burgers,* seasoned with the flavors of Mexico and topped with a re-freshing lettuce and cheese garnish? Corn chips on the side make an unbeatable combination.

Skilletburgers

1 pound ground beef
1 cup chopped onion
½ cup chopped celery
1 15-ounce can tomato sauce
½ cup water
2 tablespoons quick-cooking
    rolled oats
1 teaspoon salt
1 teaspoon Worcestershire sauce
½ teaspoon chili powder
⅛ teaspoon pepper
    Dash bottled hot pepper sauce
14 to 16 hamburger buns, split
    and toasted

In skillet cook beef, onion, and celery till beef is brown and onion is tender; drain off excess fat.

Stir in tomato sauce, water, quick-cooking rolled oats, salt, Worcestershire sauce, chili powder, pepper, and hot pepper sauce.

Simmer, uncovered, till mixture is of desired consistency, about 30 minutes. Spoon about ¼ cup meat mixture into each bun. Makes 14 to 16 sandwiches.

4 More-for-Your-Money Beef

Make the most of your meat budget with the recipes in this chapter. Discover tasty variations for using leftovers, for tenderizing cheaper cuts like stew meat and short ribs, and for serving variety meats. You can also save with more expensive cuts. Stretch the number of servings by cutting a roast or steak into cubes or strips and serving as kabobs or in combination dishes.

Help your meat budget by stretching a beef chuck roast into 8-serving *Beef Bourguignonne*. Burgundy and cognac combine to give everyday beef stew ingredients a company-special flavor.

Beef Combinations

Beef Bourguignonne

3 slices bacon, cut into small
 pieces
¼ cup cooking oil
⅓ cup all-purpose flour
2 teaspoons salt
¼ teaspoon pepper
3 pounds boneless beef chuck,
 cut into 1-inch pieces
2 medium onions, chopped
1 clove garlic, minced
¼ cup cognac *or* brandy
1 cup Burgundy
1 cup beef broth
2 bay leaves
8 small carrots, cut up
½ pound tiny onions
16 medium mushroom caps
 (2 ounces)
 Snipped parsley
 Hot cooked noodles *or*
 boiled potatoes

In 5-quart Dutch oven cook bacon till crisp; remove bacon and set aside. Add oil to bacon drippings. Combine flour, salt, and pepper; toss beef cubes with flour mixture to coat. Cook *half* the beef, the chopped onions, and garlic in the hot oil mixture till beef is brown and onions are tender; remove and set aside.

Cook remaining beef in the hot oil mixture till brown. Drain off excess fat. Return beef-onion mixture to Dutch oven. In small saucepan heat cognac or brandy; set aflame and pour over beef. Stir in Burgundy, beef broth, and bay leaves. Bring to boiling; reduce heat. Cover and simmer about 1 hour or till meat is nearly tender. Add carrots and tiny onions. Cook 20 minutes more. Add mushrooms; cook about 10 minutes more or till meat and vegetables are tender. Remove bay leaves. Stir in cooked bacon. Garnish with snipped parsley. Serve with cooked noodles or potatoes. Makes 8 servings.

Tyrolean Alps Ragout

 Brown Sauce
3 tablespoons butter *or*
 margarine
1 cup sliced fresh mushrooms
1 cup chopped onion
2 pounds beef tenderloin,
 sliced in thin strips
¼ cup dry sherry
¼ teaspoon salt
¼ teaspoon Worcestershire sauce
 Dash pepper
 Hot cooked rice

Prepare Brown Sauce. Meanwhile, in 12-inch skillet melt butter. Add mushrooms and onion; cook and stir over medium heat till tender but not brown. Push vegetables to one side of skillet. Quickly brown meat, ⅓ at a time, in butter. When all meat is browned, stir in Brown Sauce, dry sherry, salt, Worcestershire, and pepper. Heat through, 5 to 10 minutes. Serve over rice. Makes 6 to 8 servings.

Brown Sauce: In saucepan melt 2 tablespoons butter; blend in 2 tablespoons all-purpose flour. Cook and stir over medium heat till lightly browned, 2 to 3 minutes. Remove from heat; stir in one 10½-ounce can condensed beef broth and 1 cup water. Cook and stir till thickened and bubbly. Simmer, uncovered, 30 minutes; stir occasionally.

Beef Stroganoff

1 pound beef tenderloin
3 tablespoons cooking oil
1½ cups sliced fresh mushrooms
 (4 ounces)
½ cup dry sherry
¼ cup beef broth
1 cup dairy sour cream
½ teaspoon salt
 Hot cooked fine noodles

Cut tenderloin in ¼-inch-thick strips. In skillet heat oil; brown meat strips quickly in hot oil, 2 to 4 minutes. Remove meat from skillet. Add sliced mushrooms and cook 2 to 3 minutes; remove mushrooms.

Add sherry and beef broth to skillet; bring to boiling. Cook, uncovered, till liquid is reduced to ⅓ cup. Stir in sour cream and salt; stir in meat and mushrooms. Cook slowly till heated through; *do not boil.* Serve over hot cooked noodles. Makes 4 servings.

Pepper Steak, Oriental

1½ **pounds boneless beef round**
   tip, cut in ½-inch slices
 3 **tablespoons soy sauce**
 1 **tablespoon cooking oil**
   Dash freshly ground pepper
½ **teaspoon grated gingerroot** *or*
   ground ginger
 1 **clove garlic, minced**
 1 **tablespoon cooking oil**
 1 **medium green pepper, sliced**
 2 **cups sliced fresh mushrooms,**
   (about 5 ounces)
 6 **green onions with tops, cut in**
   ½-inch pieces
½ **cup beef broth**
 1 **tablespoon cornstarch**
 2 **medium tomatoes, cut in**
   wedges
   Hot cooked rice

Partially freeze beef slices; cut diagonally into ¼-inch strips. In large bowl combine soy sauce, 1 tablespoon oil, and pepper. Add beef; toss to coat well. Let stand several hours in refrigerator. Drain beef, reserving marinade.

In wok or skillet heat ginger and garlic in 1 tablespoon oil. Add beef; stir-fry till beef is browned, about 4 minutes. Remove beef with slotted spoon. Add green pepper, mushrooms, and onions to wok. Cook and stir till vegetables are crisp-tender, about 2 minutes; return beef to wok.

Combine reserved marinade, beef broth, and cornstarch; pour over beef mixture. Cook and stir till thickened and bubbly. Add tomatoes; cover and cook till heated through, about 2 minutes. Serve with rice. Makes 6 servings.

Rainbow Beef (pictured on page 4)

 1 **pound beef tenderloin** *or*
   sirloin
 1 **egg white**
 1 **tablespoon cornstarch**
 2 **cloves garlic, minced**
½ **teaspoon grated gingerroot**
½ **cup peanut** *or* **cooking**
   oil
 1 **6-ounce package frozen pea**
   pods
 2 **cups sliced fresh mushrooms,**
   (about 5 ounces)
 2 **carrots, cut in thin sticks**
   about 3 inches long
 2 **ribs celery, cut in thin**
   sticks about 3 inches long
 1 **onion, cut in thin wedges**
 1 **red pepper, cut in thin strips**
 2 **teaspoons instant chicken**
   bouillon granules
¼ **cup soy sauce**
¼ **cup cold water**
 3 **tablespoons dry sherry**
 1 **tablespoon dark corn syrup**
 1 **tablespoon vinegar**
 4 **teaspoons cornstarch**
⅛ **teaspoon freshly ground pepper**

Slice beef in thin strips. In large bowl combine egg white and 1 tablespoon cornstarch; stir in beef strips. In large wok or skillet stir-fry meat, garlic, and gingerroot in *3 tablespoons* of the hot oil till meat is browned. Remove meat from pan; set aside.

Add remaining oil to pan juices; stir in pea pods, mushrooms, carrots, celery, onion, and red pepper. Sprinkle bouillon granules over vegetable mixture. Cover and simmer till vegetables are crisp-tender, about 10 minutes.

Combine soy sauce, water, sherry, corn syrup, vinegar, 4 teaspoons cornstarch, and ground pepper. Stir mixture into vegetables along with cooked meat; cook and stir till thickened and bubbly. Makes 4 to 6 servings.

Stir-fry marinated strips of beef with fresh mushrooms, green pepper, green onions, and tomatoes to create *Pepper Steak, Oriental*. Add the thickened soy marinade for a final touch.

Beef Steak Pie

1½ pounds beef round steak,
    cut in 1-inch cubes
¼ cup all-purpose flour
1 large onion, cut in pieces
2 tablespoons lard *or* shortening
2 cups water
1 teaspoon salt
¼ teaspoon dried thyme, crushed
⅛ teaspoon pepper
2 cups diced raw potato
    Pastry Topper
    Salt
    Pepper
    Milk

Toss beef with flour. In saucepan cook beef and onion in lard till beef is browned and onion is tender. Add water, 1 teaspoon salt, thyme, and ⅛ teaspoon pepper. Cover; simmer 1½ hours. Add potato. Cover; simmer 20 minutes.

Prepare Pastry Topper. Turn meat into a 1½-quart casserole; season with salt and pepper. Cut slits in pastry; place over hot mixture. Turn under edge; flute. Brush with milk. Bake at 450° till golden, about 15 minutes. Serves 6.

Pastry Topper: Combine ¾ cup all-purpose flour and ¼ teaspoon salt. Cut in ¼ cup lard *or* shortening till pieces are size of small peas. Using 2 to 3 tablespoons cold water, sprinkle 1 tablespoon at a time over mixture; gently toss with fork. Form into a ball. Roll on lightly floured surface to a circle, ½ to 1 inch larger than casserole.

Stroganoff Steakwiches

¼ cup butter *or* margarine
1 large onion, sliced and
    separated into rings
¾ cup sliced fresh mushrooms
¾ pound beef round steak, cut
    in thin strips
1 cup dairy sour cream
1 teaspoon sugar
½ teaspoon salt
½ teaspoon dry mustard
4 Kaiser rolls *or* hamburger
    buns, split, toasted, and
    buttered
    Paprika

In 10-inch skillet melt butter. Cook onion and mushrooms in butter till tender but not brown; push vegetables to one side of skillet. Add steak strips; cook and stir over medium-high heat till steak is browned.

Blend together sour cream, sugar, salt, and dry mustard. Stir into steak mixture in skillet. Heat through over low heat; *do not boil*. Spoon stroganoff over toasted and buttered rolls; sprinkle with paprika. Makes 4 servings.

Greek-Style Sandwiches

½ cup dry red wine
2 tablespoons olive *or* cooking
    oil
1 small clove garlic, minced
½ teaspoon dried oregano,
    crushed
½ teaspoon salt
    Dash freshly ground pepper
1 pound beef sirloin steak, cut
    ½ inch thick
1 tablespoon butter *or* margarine
4 or 5 pieces pita pocket bread
2 cups chopped lettuce
1 large tomato, seeded and
    diced (1 cup)
1 small cucumber, seeded and
    diced (⅔ cup)
1 8-ounce container sour cream
    dip with chives (1 cup)

Combine wine, oil, garlic, oregano, salt, and pepper. Cut steak into strips, 2 inches long and ¼ inch wide. Pour wine mixture over beef. Cover; refrigerate up to 24 hours.

Thoroughly drain beef. In medium skillet brown beef, half at a time, on all sides in hot butter, 2 to 3 minutes.

With sharp knife, open one side of each piece of bread to make a pocket. Fill each pocket with a little of the beef, chopped lettuce, diced tomato, diced cucumber, and sour cream dip with chives. Makes 4 or 5 sandwiches.

Artichokes Stroganoff

2 cups sliced fresh mushrooms
   (about 5 ounces)
¼ cup chopped onion
6 tablespoons butter *or*
   margarine
1½ pounds boneless beef chuck,
   cubed
1½ cups beef broth
1 tablespoon chili sauce
¼ teaspoon salt
   Dash pepper
6 artichokes
1 cup dairy sour cream
2 tablespoons all-purpose flour

In medium skillet cook mushrooms and onion in *4 table-spoons* of the butter till tender but not brown; remove from skillet. In same skillet brown beef in remaining butter; stir in mushroom mixture, beef broth, chili sauce, salt, and pepper. Cover; simmer till meat is tender, about 1 hour.

Meanwhile, with sharp knife cut off artichoke stems; slice off about 1 inch from top of each artichoke. Remove and discard all coarse outer leaves. Snip off sharp leaf tips with kitchen shears. Place artichokes in boiling, salted water. Cover and simmer till stalks are tender or leaves can easily be pulled from base, about 20 minutes. Remove artichokes and invert to drain.

Using a melon-ball cutter or a sharp-edged spoon, thoroughly scoop out fuzzy choke and enough of the center leaves to make a generous hollow. Set artichokes aside; keep warm.

Combine sour cream and flour. Gradually blend some of the hot beef mixture into sour cream; return to skillet. Cook and stir over low heat till thickened and hot; *do not boil.*

Spoon meat and mushroom mixture into artichokes. To eat, tear off artichoke leaves; dip into sauce. Serves 6.

Tamales

2 pounds boneless beef chuck,
   cubed
3 tablespoons cooking oil
¼ cup all-purpose flour
1 cup Red Chili Sauce
6 tablespoons finely chopped
   canned green chili peppers
1½ teaspoons salt
¼ teaspoon dried oregano,
   crushed
2 cloves garlic, minced
   Cornhusks, parchment, *or* foil
1½ cups lard
1½ teaspoons salt
4½ cups masa harina
2⅔ cups warm water

In saucepan simmer beef in enough water to cover till meat is well done, about 1½ hours. Drain; reserve 1½ cups liquid.

Shred meat; brown in hot oil. Stir in flour; cook and stir till flour is browned. Stir in reserved cooking liquid, Red Chili Sauce, chili peppers, the 1½ teaspoons salt, oregano, and garlic. Simmer, covered, about 30 minutes.

For tamale wrappers, soak cornhusks in warm water several hours or overnight to soften. Overlap cornhusks as necessary to make twelve 8x8-inch wrappers. (Or use squares of parchment or foil.)

With electric mixer cream lard with the 1½ teaspoons salt. Combine masa harina and warm water; beat into lard. Place ½ cup of the dough in center of each tamale wrapper. Spread dough evenly to a 6x5-inch rectangle.

Spoon about ⅓ *cup* of the meat mixture down center of each dough rectangle. Lift two opposite sides of wrapper toward center till edges of dough meet. Gently peel back wrapper; seal dough edges to enclose. Overlap the two sides of wrapper over dough. Tie wrapper ends tightly with string. (For foil, fold ends under, or twist to seal.)

Place tamales on rack in large steamer or electric skillet. Add water to just below rack. Cover; steam 1½ hours, adding water when needed. Makes 12.

Red Chili Sauce: In saucepan melt 2 tablespoons shortening. Stir in 2 tablespoons all-purpose flour. Add ¼ cup chili powder, stirring till completely moistened. Gradually stir in 1 cup water; stir till chili powder is dissolved, making sure no lumps form. Stir in one 8-ounce can tomato sauce, ½ teaspoon garlic salt, and ½ teaspoon salt. Cover; simmer 15 minutes. Makes about 2 cups.

Steak and Vegetable Kabobs

1 cup Burgundy
¼ cup cooking oil
2 tablespoons onion soup mix
1 teaspoon salt
½ teaspoon dried thyme, crushed
¼ teaspoon pepper
1 small clove garlic, minced
2 pounds beef sirloin steak,
    cut in 1-inch pieces
2 zucchini, cut in 1-inch slices
2 ears corn, cut in 1-inch
    slices
    Cherry tomatoes

In bowl combine Burgundy, oil, dry onion soup mix, salt, thyme, pepper, and garlic. Add meat; stir to coat. Cover; marinate at room temperature 2 hours, or overnight in refrigerator. Drain meat, reserving marinade.

Sprinkle zucchini and corn with salt. Using 6 skewers, thread meat alternately on skewers with zucchini and corn.

Place kabobs on cold rack of broiler pan; broil 4 to 6 inches from heat till all sides are browned, allowing 8 minutes total broiling time. Give kabobs a quarter turn every 2 minutes, brushing with a little of the reserved marinade. Add a cherry tomato to each skewer. Serve over rice and trim with parsley, if desired. Makes 6 servings.

Beer Beef Kabobs

1 pound boneless beef sirloin,
    cut in 1½-inch cubes
1 12-ounce bottle dark *or* light
    beer (1½ cups)
¼ cup diced onion
2 tablespoons cooking oil
1 teaspoon salt
1 teaspoon curry powder
½ teaspoon ground ginger
    Dash garlic powder
    Large whole fresh mushrooms
    Green pepper squares

Place beef cubes in shallow dish. Combine beer, onion, oil, salt, curry powder, ginger, and garlic powder; pour over beef. Marinate 3 hours at room temperature.

Drain meat, reserving marinade. Using 3 or 4 skewers, thread meat alternately on skewers with mushrooms and pepper pieces. Place kabobs on cold rack of broiler pan.

Broil kabobs 3 to 4 inches from heat, 7 to 8 minutes; brush with a little of the reserved marinade. Turn; broil kabobs 3 to 4 minutes longer, brushing often with reserved marinade. Makes 3 or 4 servings.

Fondue Wellington

1½ pounds beef tenderloin,
    trimmed and cut in 1-inch
    cubes
1 medium onion, sliced
⅔ cup red wine vinegar
⅓ cup water
¼ cup catsup
2 tablespoons soy sauce
½ teaspoon dry mustard
1 small clove garlic, minced
2 packages refrigerated crescent
    rolls (8 rolls each)
1 4¾-ounce can liver spread
    Cooking oil
1 teaspoon salt

In skillet cook beef, uncovered, over medium-high heat to medium doneness, 12 minutes; turn occasionally. Drain.

Combine onion, vinegar, water, catsup, soy sauce, dry mustard, and garlic; add meat. Cover and chill several hours or overnight, stirring mixture occasionally.

Two hours before serving, drain meat; reserve marinade. For *each* package of rolls, separate dough into 4 rectangles; pinch together well along perforations. Spread a little of the liver spread on *each* rectangle. Cut *each* rectangle in half lengthwise, then crosswise. Place a meat cube on *each* quarter of dough; fold dough over meat and seal. Let stand at room temperature.

Pour oil into fondue cooker to no more than ½ capacity or to depth of 2 inches. Heat over range to 375°. Add salt; transfer to fondue burner. Using fondue forks, cook meat in hot oil 2 to 2½ minutes. (Temperature of oil will drop during cooking; adjust heat accordingly.) Strain reserved marinade and heat; use for dipping. Makes 32.

Marinated sirloin chunks are skewered with corn-on-the-cob, zucchini, and tomatoes in *Steak and Vegetable Kabobs.* Brush the Burgundy-onion marinade over the kabobs during broiling.

Soup and Stew Specialties

Cider Stew (pictured on cover)

3 tablespoons all-purpose flour
2 teaspoons salt
¼ teaspoon pepper
¼ teaspoon dried thyme, crushed
2 pounds beef stew meat
3 tablespoons cooking oil
2 cups apple cider
½ cup water
2 tablespoons vinegar
4 carrots, quartered
3 potatoes, peeled and quartered
2 onions, sliced
1 rib celery, sliced
1 apple, chopped

Combine flour, salt, pepper, and thyme; toss with meat to coat. In Dutch oven brown meat in hot oil. Stir in cider, water, and vinegar; cook and stir to boiling. Reduce heat; simmer, covered, till meat is tender, 1½ to 2 hours.

Add vegetables and apple. Cook till vegetables are tender, about 30 minutes. Makes 6 to 8 servings.

Crockery cooker directions: Use ingredients as above, *except* do not add water, use only 1 tablespoon of vinegar, and chop the vegetables. Combine flour, salt, pepper, and thyme; toss with meat to coat. In large skillet or saucepan brown the meat in hot oil. Place *chopped* vegetables in electric slow crockery cooker. Add apple and meat. Combine cider and *only 1 tablespoon* vinegar; do *not* add water. Pour over meat and vegetables. Cover; cook on low-heat setting for 10 to 12 hours.

Turn cooker to high-heat setting. Blend ½ cup cold water with ¼ cup all-purpose flour; stir into stew. Cover and cook till thickened, about 15 minutes. Season to taste with salt and pepper. Serve as above.

Oxtail Stew

⅓ cup all-purpose flour
1 teaspoon salt
¼ teaspoon pepper
3 pounds oxtails, cut in
    2½-inch pieces
2 tablespoons cooking oil
6 carrots, cut in 1-inch pieces
1 cup chopped onion
1 cup chopped celery
1 clove garlic, minced
2½ cups beef broth
2 tablespoons tomato paste
1 bay leaf, broken
¼ teaspoon dried thyme, crushed

Combine flour, salt, and pepper; coat oxtails with flour mixture. In Dutch oven brown oxtails, half at a time, in hot oil. Remove oxtails; drain, reserving 2 tablespoons oil.

In reserved oil cook carrots, onion, celery, and garlic till onion and celery are tender. Stir in beef broth, tomato paste, bay leaf, and thyme; bring mixture to boiling. Add oxtails. Cover; simmer till tender, 2 to 2½ hours. Skim off excess fat before serving. Makes 4 servings.

Bronco Buster Soup

1¼ cups dry pinto beans (½ pound)
6 cups water
1 1-pound beef shank
1 cup chopped onion
2 teaspoons salt
½ teaspoon dried thyme, crushed
    Dash pepper
2 medium potatoes, peeled and
    diced (2 cups)
2 medium carrots, sliced (1 cup)

Rinse beans. Place in large saucepan and add 6 cups water. Soak overnight. (Or, bring beans to boiling; reduce heat and simmer 2 minutes. Remove from heat. Cover; let stand 1 hour.) Do not drain. Add beef shank, onion, salt, thyme, and pepper; bring mixture to boiling. Reduce heat; simmer, covered, 1¼ hours, stirring occasionally.

Remove shank; cool. Cut off meat and dice; discard bones. Mash beans slightly. Add meat, potatoes, and carrots to soup. Cover; simmer till vegetables are tender, about 30 minutes more. Makes 6 servings.

Simmer *Cider Stew* atop the range or in an electric slow crockery cooker. Either way this tasty stew is a hearty meal-in-a-dish with the special flavor of cider and chopped apple.

Basic Beef Stock

  4 **pounds meaty beef bones**
  3 **medium onions, quartered**
1½ **cups celery leaves**
  6 **sprigs parsley**
  4 or 5 **whole peppercorns**
  2 or 3 **bay leaves**
  1 or 2 **cloves garlic, halved**
  1 **tablespoon salt**
  2 **teaspoons dried thyme,**
     crushed *or* 1 **tablespoon**
     dried basil, crushed
10 **cups water**
     Use any 2 or 3 of the following
     vegetable trimmings (approximate
     measures):
        1½ **cups potato peelings**
        1½ **cups carrot peelings**
        1½ **cups turnip tops** *or*
           peelings
        1½ **cups parsnip tops** *or*
           peelings (wax removed)
        4 or 5 **outer leaves**
           of cabbage.
        ¾ **cup sliced green onion tops**
        ¾ **cup sliced leek tops**
  1 **eggshell, crushed**
  1 **egg white**
¼ **cup water**

In 10-quart Dutch oven combine bones, quartered onions, celery leaves, parsley, peppercorns, bay leaves, garlic, salt, and thyme or basil. Add 10 cups water and *2 or 3* of the vegetable trimmings, using only approximate measures for trimmings. Bring to boiling. Cover; simmer 2½ to 3 hours.

Remove meat and bones; set aside. Strain stock, discarding vegetables and herbs. To clarify stock, combine eggshell, egg white, and ¼ cup water. Stir into hot stock; bring to boiling. Remove from heat; let stand 5 minutes.

Strain stock through cheesecloth. Skim off excess fat or chill and lift off fat. Pour stock into pint or quart jars or containers; cover and chill. (Store stock in refrigerator up to 2 weeks or in freezer up to 6 months.) Use stock in any recipe that calls for beef broth or serve alone.

When bones are cool, remove meat from bones. Store meat in separate covered container in refrigerator or wrap in moisture-vaporproof freezer wrap; seal, label, and freeze. Use meat in soups or stews. Makes 7 to 8 cups.

Texas-Style Chili

2¼ **pounds beef round steak,**
     cut in cubes
  1 **clove garlic, minced**
  3 **tablespoons cooking oil**
1½ **cups water**
  1 **10½-ounce can condensed beef**
     broth
  2 **teaspoons sugar**
  2 **teaspoons dried oregano,**
     crushed
  1 to 2 **teaspoons cumin seed,**
     crushed
½ **teaspoon salt**
  2 **bay leaves**
  1 **4-ounce can green chili**
     peppers, drained, seeded,
     and chopped
  2 **tablespoons cornmeal**
     Corn bread (optional)

In large skillet brown steak cubes and garlic in hot oil; drain off excess fat. Stir in water, condensed beef broth, sugar, oregano, cumin, salt, and bay leaves. Reduce heat; simmer, covered, till meat is tender, about 1½ hours.

Stir in chili peppers and cornmeal. Simmer, covered, 30 minutes; stir occasionally. Remove bay leaves. Serve over squares of corn bread, if desired. Makes 4 to 6 servings.

Beef Shank-Vegetable Soup

3 pounds beef shank cross cuts
2 tablespoons cooking oil
4 cups water
1 16-ounce can tomatoes, cut up
1 10¾-ounce can condensed
    tomato soup
⅓ cup chopped onion
1 tablespoon salt
2 teaspoons Worcestershire sauce
¼ teaspoon chili powder
2 bay leaves
1 16-ounce can lima beans,
    drained
2 medium carrots, thinly sliced
1 medium potato, peeled and
    diced
1 cup chopped celery
1 8¾-ounce can whole kernel corn

In Dutch oven brown shanks on both sides in hot oil; add water, undrained tomatoes, soup, onion, salt, Worcestershire, chili powder, and bay leaves. Bring to boiling; reduce heat. Simmer, covered, 2 hours; stir occasionally.

Remove shanks; cool. Cut off meat and dice; discard bones. Skim fat from soup. Add meat, limas, carrots, potato, celery, and undrained corn to soup. Cover; simmer till done, about 45 minutes. Discard bay leaves. Makes 12 servings.

Crockery cooker directions: Use ingredients as above, *except* use only 3 cups water. In skillet brown shanks in hot oil; transfer to electric slow crockery cooker. Add *only 3 cups* water, undrained tomatoes, soup, onion, salt, Worcestershire, chili powder, and bay leaves. Cover; cook on low-heat setting for 4 hours.

Turn cooker to high-heat setting. Remove shanks; discard bay leaves. Skim fat from soup. Stir in limas, carrots, potato, celery, and undrained corn. Cover and continue cooking. Cut meat from bone; dice and return to cooker. Cover; cook 2 to 3 hours longer.

Pease Soup

8 cups water
1 pound dry green split peas
    (2¼ cups)
1 pound beef stew meat, cut in
    ½-inch cubes
½ pound salt pork
1 cup chopped onion
½ teaspoon salt
½ teaspoon dried basil, crushed
¼ teaspoon dried marjoram,
    crushed
⅛ teaspoon pepper
3 cups chopped fresh spinach *or*
    sorrel
2 cups sliced celery
¾ teaspoon dried mint leaves,
    crushed

In large Dutch oven combine water, peas, beef cubes, salt pork, chopped onion, salt, basil, marjoram, and pepper. Bring mixture to boiling; cover and reduce heat. Simmer till beef is barely tender, about 1½ hours.

Remove and discard salt pork. Mash pea mixture slightly. Add spinach or sorrel, celery, and mint. Cover; cook till meat and celery are tender, about 30 minutes more. If desired, top with croutons before serving. Makes 8 servings.

Cutting Stew Meat

Stretch your meat budget further by cutting round steak or large pot roasts into stew meat and meal-sized roasts. For stew meat, trim away the bone and excess fat; then cut meat into 1- to 2-inch cubes. Try to keep them as uniformly shaped as possible so they will cook evenly.

If you want to make two meals from one roast, divide a 4- to 5-pound beef blade pot roast. Cut at the end of the bone, separating the square bone-in piece from the triangular boneless piece. Cut the boneless portion for stew meat. Cook the bone-in piece as a pot roast.

Ladle *Sweet-Sour Beef Stew* over poppy seed noodles for a snappy variation of the common stew. Flecked with carrot, this slow-cooking combination is equally tasty served over rice.

Sweet-Sour Beef Stew

1½ **pounds beef stew meat, cut in**
    1-inch cubes
  2 **tablespoons cooking oil**
  2 **medium carrots, shredded**
    (1 cup)
  2 **medium onions, sliced**
    (1 cup)
  1 **8-ounce can tomato sauce**
 ½ **cup water**
 ¼ **cup packed brown sugar**
 ¼ **cup vinegar**
  1 **tablespoon Worcestershire**
    sauce
  1 **teaspoon salt**
  1 **tablespoon cold water**
  2 **teaspoons cornstarch**
    Hot cooked noodles
    Poppy seed (optional)

In 3-quart saucepan brown meat, half at a time, in hot oil. In same saucepan combine meat, shredded carrot, sliced onion, tomato sauce, ½ cup water, brown sugar, vinegar, Worcestershire, and salt. Cover and cook over low heat till meat is tender, about 1½ hours.

Blend 1 tablespoon cold water with cornstarch; add to stew. Cook and stir till thickened and bubbly. Serve stew over noodles sprinkled with poppy seed. Garnish with carrot curls and parsley, if desired. Makes 4 to 6 servings.

Oven-Baked Beef Stew

¼ **cup all-purpose flour**
2 **teaspoons salt**
⅛ **teaspoon pepper**
1½ **pounds beef stew meat, cut in
    1-inch cubes**
3 **to 4 medium carrots, cut in
    2-inch strips**
4 **small onions, quartered**
2 **cups water**
1 **6-ounce can tomato paste**
1 **tablespoon vinegar**
1 **teaspoon sugar**
⅛ **teaspoon dried thyme, crushed**
1 **clove garlic, minced**
1 **bay leaf**
1 **10-ounce package frozen peas,
    broken apart**
1 **package refrigerated biscuits
    (6 biscuits)**
  Milk
¼ **cup crisp rice cereal,
    crushed**

In paper or plastic bag combine flour, salt, and pepper. Add beef cubes, ¼ at a time; shake to coat. Place beef cubes in a 2½- or 3-quart casserole; add carrots and onions. In bowl combine water, tomato paste, vinegar, sugar, thyme, garlic, and bay leaf; pour over meat mixture in casserole. Bake, covered, at 350° for 2 hours.

Stir frozen peas into stew mixture; cover and bake 20 minutes longer. Remove casserole from oven; discard bay leaf. Increase oven temperature to 425°.

Meanwhile, quarter biscuits; dip in milk, then roll in cereal. Place atop hot stew. Bake, uncovered, at 425° till biscuits are done, about 12 minutes. Makes 6 servings.

Estofado

1 **pound beef stew meat, cut in
    1-inch cubes**
1 **tablespoon cooking oil**
1 **cup dry red wine**
1 **8-ounce can tomatoes, cut up**
1 **large onion, sliced ¼ inch
    thick**
1 **green pepper, cut in
    strips**
¼ **cup raisins**
¼ **cup dried apricots, halved**
1½ **teaspoons salt**
⅛ **teaspoon pepper**
1 **clove garlic, minced**
1 **teaspoon dried basil**
1 **teaspoon dried thyme**
1 **teaspoon dried tarragon**
1 **bay leaf**
½ **cup sliced fresh mushrooms**
¼ **cup sliced pitted ripe
    olives**
1 **cup cold water**
1 **tablespoon all-purpose flour**
  Hot cooked rice

In 10-inch skillet brown beef cubes in hot oil. Stir in wine, undrained tomatoes, onion, green pepper, raisins, apricots, salt, pepper, and garlic. In a cheesecloth bag combine basil, thyme, tarragon, and bay leaf; add to meat mixture. Simmer, covered, 1 hour.

Stir mushrooms and olives into stew; simmer, covered, 30 minutes more. Discard herb bag. Blend cold water with flour; stir into stew. Cook and stir till thickened and bubbly. Serve over rice. Makes 6 servings.

Short Ribs that Satisfy

Short Ribs with Cornmeal Dumplings

3 pounds beef short ribs, cut
    in serving-size pieces
Salt
Pepper
1 medium onion, cut in thin
    wedges
1 clove garlic, minced
1 28-ounce can tomatoes, cut up
1 12-ounce can beer
1 fresh *or* dried hot red chili
    pepper, seeded and chopped
2 tablespoons soy sauce
1 tablespoon sugar
¾ teaspoon salt
¼ teaspoon pepper
¼ teaspoon ground nutmeg
    Cornmeal Dumplings

Trim excess fat from ribs. In Dutch oven brown ribs on all sides; season with salt and pepper. Remove ribs. Drain off fat, reserving about 2 tablespoons drippings in pan.

Cook onion and garlic in reserved drippings till onion is tender. Add undrained tomatoes, beer, chili pepper, soy, sugar, ¾ teaspoon salt, ¼ teaspoon pepper, and nutmeg. Return meat to Dutch oven; bring to boiling. Reduce heat; simmer, covered, till meat is tender, 1½ to 2 hours.

Cool meat mixture; skim off excess fat. Return to heat; bring to boiling. Meanwhile, prepare Cornmeal Dumplings. Drop batter by rounded tablespoonfuls onto boiling meat mixture. Cover; simmer till dumplings are done, 10 to 12 minutes. Makes 6 to 8 servings.

Cornmeal Dumplings: In saucepan combine 1 cup water, ½ cup yellow cornmeal, and ½ teaspoon salt. Bring to boiling; cook and stir till thickened. Remove from heat. Stir a moderate amount of hot mixture into 1 beaten egg; return to hot mixture. Stir ½ cup all-purpose flour with 1 teaspoon baking powder and dash pepper. Add to cornmeal mixture; beat well. Drain one 7-ounce can whole kernel corn; fold in.

Hungarian Short Ribs

4 pounds beef short ribs
2 medium onions, sliced
1 15-ounce can tomato sauce
2 cups water
¼ cup packed brown sugar
¼ cup vinegar
1½ teaspoons salt
1½ teaspoons dry mustard
1½ teaspoons Worcestershire sauce
¼ teaspoon paprika
6 ounces medium noodles
    (4½ cups)

Cut ribs in serving-size pieces; trim excess fat. In Dutch oven brown ribs on all sides. Add onions. Blend together tomato sauce, *1 cup* of the water, brown sugar, vinegar, salt, dry mustard, Worcestershire, and paprika; pour over meat. Cover and simmer till meat is almost tender, about 2 hours.

Skim off fat. Stir in noodles and remaining 1 cup water. Cover and cook, stirring occasionally, till noodles are tender, 20 to 25 minutes more. Makes 6 to 8 servings.

Cranberry Grilled Short Ribs

5½ to 6 pounds beef short ribs,
    cut in serving-size pieces
2 teaspoons salt
    Dash pepper
½ cup water
1 12-ounce jar pineapple preserves
½ cup canned whole cranberry
    sauce
½ cup chili sauce
⅓ cup vinegar

Trim excess fat from ribs; sprinkle ribs with salt and pepper. Place in Dutch oven; add water. Cover and simmer till meat is tender, about 2 hours. Add additional water during cooking if necessary.

Drain ribs. Combine preserves, cranberry sauce, chili sauce, and vinegar; brush some of the glaze mixture over ribs. Place ribs on grill; cook over *slow* coals 15 to 20 minutes, brushing ribs with glaze and turning frequently. Heat remaining glaze; pass with ribs. Makes 6 servings.

Short Ribs with Cornmeal Dumplings is hearty fare for big appetites. The short ribs simmer leisurely in a zesty broth made with tomatoes, beer, hot red chili pepper, and soy sauce.

Borsch-Style Stew (pictured on page 4)

1½ to 2 pounds beef short ribs,
    cut up
4 carrots, sliced (2 cups)
3 turnips, peeled, sliced, and
    cut in strips (1½ cups)
3 ribs celery, sliced (1 cup)
1 medium onion, sliced (1 cup)
4 cups water
1 6-ounce can tomato paste
1 tablespoon salt
¼ teaspoon pepper
1 cup water
1 tablespoon sugar
1 tablespoon vinegar
2 medium beets, peeled, sliced,
    and cut in strips (2 cups)
1 small head cabbage, cut in
    6 wedges
    Dairy sour cream

Trim excess fat from ribs. In 4½-quart Dutch oven brown ribs on all sides; drain. Add carrots, turnips, celery, and onion. Blend the 4 cups water with tomato paste, salt, and pepper; pour over meat and vegetables in Dutch oven. Cover; bake at 350° for 2 hours. Skim off fat.

Combine the 1 cup water, sugar, and vinegar; stir into meat mixture. Add beets; place cabbage wedges atop mixture, pushing partially into liquid. Cover; bake 1½ hours more. Pass sour cream to spoon atop. Makes 6 servings.

Crockery cooker directions: Use ingredients as above *except* use only 3 cups water. Trim ribs as above; brown and drain. Place carrots, turnips, celery, onion, and beets in electric slow crockery cooker; top with ribs. Combine *only 3 cups* water with tomato paste, salt, pepper, sugar, and vinegar; mix well. Pour over ribs. Cover; cook on low-heat setting 10 to 12 hours. Skim off fat.

Fifteen minutes before serving stew, cook cabbage wedges in a 3-quart saucepan in a large amount of boiling, salted water till tender, 10 to 12 minutes. Drain well. Serve with stew. Pass sour cream to top each serving.

Short Ribs with Limas

3 pounds beef short ribs, cut in
    serving-size pieces
1½ teaspoons salt
⅛ teaspoon pepper
1½ cups water
¾ cup packed brown sugar
½ cup chopped onion
⅓ cup vinegar
1½ teaspoons dry mustard
2 bay leaves
¼ cup cold water
2 teaspoons cornstarch
2 16-ounce cans lima beans,
    drained

Trim excess fat from ribs, reserving trimmings. In Dutch oven or skillet cook reserved trimmings till 2 tablespoons fat accumulate; discard remaining trimmings. Brown ribs on all sides in hot fat; drain off excess fat. Reduce heat.

Sprinkle ribs with salt and pepper; add the 1½ cups water, brown sugar, onion, vinegar, dry mustard, and bay leaves. Cover; simmer till ribs are tender, about 2 hours.

Transfer ribs to serving platter; keep hot. Discard bay leaves; spoon off fat from pan juices. Blend the ¼ cup cold water with cornstarch; stir into pan juices. Cook and stir till thickened and bubbly; stir in beans. Cover; simmer 5 to 10 minutes. Serve with ribs. Makes 6 servings.

Short Ribs with Onion Gravy

3 pounds beef short ribs, cut in
    serving-size pieces
1 teaspoon salt
    Dash pepper
3 medium onions, sliced
½ cup water
3 tablespoons sugar
3 tablespoons all-purpose flour
2 tablespoons vinegar
    Salt
    Pepper

Trim excess fat from ribs. In Dutch oven brown ribs on all sides. Sprinkle with the 1 teaspoon salt and dash pepper. Add one of the sliced onions and the ½ cup water. Cover and simmer till meat is tender, 2 to 2½ hours; add additional water, if needed.

Transfer ribs to platter; keep hot. Pour pan juices into measuring cup; skim off fat, returning 2 tablespoons fat to pan. Add water to juices to make 2 cups; set aside.

Cook and stir sugar in reserved fat till browned. Add remaining 2 sliced onions; cook and stir till onion is tender. Blend in flour. Stir in reserved pan juices and vinegar; cook and stir till thickened and bubbly. Season to taste with salt and pepper. Pass with ribs. Makes 6 servings.

Beef Barley Soup

2 pounds beef short ribs
5 cups water
1 16-ounce can tomatoes, cut up
1 large onion, sliced
1 tablespoon instant beef
   bouillon granules
2 teaspoons salt
¾ teaspoon dried basil, crushed
2 cups sliced carrot
1 cup sliced celery
¾ cup chopped green pepper
⅔ cup quick-cooking barley
¼ cup snipped parsley

In Dutch oven slowly brown short ribs on all sides; drain off excess fat. Add water, undrained tomatoes, onion, bouillon granules, salt, and basil. Simmer, covered, 1½ hours.

Add carrot, celery, green pepper, barley, and parsley. Simmer, covered, 45 minutes more. Remove meat and bones. Chop meat; discard bones. Skim excess fat from soup. Return meat to soup; heat through. Serves 8 to 10.

Crockery cooker directions: Use ingredients as above, *except* pearl barley may be substituted for the quick-cooking barley. In skillet slowly brown short ribs on all sides; drain well. Combine undrained tomatoes, barley, parsley, instant beef bouillon granules, salt, and basil; set aside. Place onion, carrot, celery, and green pepper in electric slow crockery cooker. Top with the browned ribs. Pour tomato mixture over meat in cooker. Add water; *do not stir.* Cover; cook on low-heat setting for 10 to 12 hours.

Remove bones and meat from soup; discard bones. Skim excess fat from soup. Chop meat and return to cooker. Season soup to taste with additional salt and pepper.

Savory Beef-Vegetable Soup

2 pounds beef short ribs,
   cut up
6 cups water
1 cup chopped potato
1 cup chopped onion
1 cup chopped carrot
1 cup chopped celery
1 tablespoon salt
   Dash pepper
1 16-ounce can whole kernel
   corn
1 15½-ounce can cut green beans

Trim excess fat from short ribs; place ribs in large saucepan. Add water, potato, onion, carrot, celery, salt, and pepper. Bring to boiling. Cover; simmer till beef is tender, about 2 hours. Skim off fat. Remove meat and bones, cool slightly. Chop meat and return to soup; discard bones.

Stir in undrained corn and undrained green beans. Cover and simmer about 30 minutes. Season to taste with salt and pepper. Makes 10 to 12 servings.

Crockery cooker directions: Use ingredients as above, *except* use only 3 cups water, and add 2 teaspoons beef-flavored gravy base. In electric slow crockery cooker place potato, onion, carrot, and celery. Trim fat from ribs; place atop vegetables in cooker. Sprinkle with salt and pepper. Stir together only 3 cups water and 2 teaspoons beef-flavored gravy base; pour over beef.

Cover and cook on low-heat setting for 10 to 12 hours. Turn to high-heat setting. Remove ribs; skim off fat. Stir in the undrained corn and undrained green beans. Cover and cook 30 minutes longer. Meanwhile, chop meat and return to soup; discard bones. Season to taste with salt and pepper. Cover and cook 5 minutes more. Stir soup before serving.

Broiled Short Ribs

4 pounds beef short ribs, cut up
⅔ cup catsup
¼ cup light molasses
¼ cup lemon juice
1 tablespoon dry mustard
½ teaspoon chili powder
   Dash garlic powder

Trim fat from ribs. Sprinkle with some salt and pepper. Place ribs in Dutch oven; add water to cover. Simmer, covered, till meat is tender, about 2 hours. Drain; place ribs on rack of broiler pan. Blend catsup, molasses, lemon juice, dry mustard, chili powder, and garlic powder; brush some over ribs. Broil 4 to 5 inches from heat for 10 to 15 minutes; turn often, basting with sauce. Makes 4 servings.

Variety Meats for a Change

Mexican-Style Liver

6 slices bacon
¾ cup chopped onion
1 clove garlic, minced
¼ cup all-purpose flour
1½ teaspoons chili powder
1 teaspoon salt
1½ pounds beef liver
1 16-ounce can tomatoes, cut up
1 12-ounce can whole kernel corn, drained
Tortillas *or* hot cooked rice

In large skillet cook bacon till crisp. Drain, reserving 3 tablespoons drippings in skillet. Crumble bacon; set aside. Cook onion and garlic in reserved drippings till onion is tender but not brown, about 5 minutes.

Combine flour, chili powder, and salt. Cut liver into thin strips; toss with flour mixture to coat. Add liver to onion in skillet; brown quickly on all sides. Stir in crumbled bacon, undrained tomatoes, and whole kernel corn. Simmer, covered, till mixture is heated through. Serve with tortillas or over hot cooked rice. Makes 6 servings.

Sautéed Liver

1 cup sliced onion
2 tablespoons shortening
4 slices beef liver, cut ⅜ inch thick (about 1 pound)
2 teaspoons lemon juice
1 teaspoon Worcestershire sauce

In skillet cook onion in hot shortening till tender but not brown; remove from skillet. Add liver; sprinkle with some salt and pepper. Cook 3 minutes at medium heat; turn. Return onion to skillet; cook 3 minutes more. Transfer liver and onion to serving platter. Blend lemon juice and Worcestershire into pan drippings; pour over liver. Makes 4 servings.

Liver Barbecue

4 slices bacon
1½ pounds beef liver, sliced
1 large onion, cut in thin wedges
1 clove garlic, minced
1 15½-ounce can barbecue-flavor sandwich sauce
¾ cup water
1 tablespoon horseradish mustard
Hot cooked noodles

In large skillet cook bacon till crisp; drain, reserving 3 tablespoons drippings in skillet. Crumble bacon; set aside. In reserved drippings brown liver quickly on both sides; remove and cut into strips. In same skillet cook onion and garlic till tender but not brown. Stir in sandwich sauce, water, and mustard. Season with some salt and pepper.

Return liver and crumbled bacon to skillet. Simmer, uncovered, till liver is tender, about 10 minutes. Serve over hot cooked noodles. Makes 6 servings.

Heart and Rice Skillet

1 1½-pound beef heart
2 tablespoons cooking oil
1½ cups water
⅔ cup regular rice
⅓ cup chopped celery
¼ cup chopped green pepper
1 3-ounce can sliced mushrooms
1 10¾-ounce can condensed cream of mushroom soup
½ envelope onion soup mix (about ¼ cup)

Rinse heart; remove outer membrane. Slit heart open; remove hard parts from center. Trim fat from heart; discard. Cut heart into ½-inch cubes. In 10-inch skillet brown meat in hot cooking oil. Add water; cover and simmer till meat is nearly tender, about 45 minutes.

Add uncooked rice, celery, and green pepper to skillet; bring to boiling. Reduce heat; cover and simmer till rice is tender, about 20 minutes. Drain mushrooms; stir into heart mixture with the mushroom soup and dry onion soup mix; heat through. Makes 6 servings.

Surprise your family with green pepper-trimmed *Mexican-Style Liver*. This south-of-the-border version of traditional liver and onions adds corn, tomatoes, bacon, and chili powder.

Heart and Stuffing

1   1½-pound beef heart
1   13¾-ounce can chicken broth
1   bay leaf
1   cup chopped celery
¼   cup chopped onion
3   tablespoons butter
4   cups coarsely crumbled corn
      bread
2   cups dry bread cubes
      (4 slices bread)
1   10-ounce package frozen mixed
      vegetables, cooked and
      drained
1   teaspoon ground sage
½   teaspoon salt
1   10¾-ounce can condensed
      golden mushroom soup
¼   cup water

Rinse heart; remove outer membrane. Slit heart open; remove hard parts from center. Place heart in Dutch oven; add chicken broth and bay leaf. Cover and simmer till meat is tender, about 2½ hours.

Meanwhile, cook celery and onion in butter till tender. In large bowl combine corn bread crumbs, bread cubes, mixed vegetables, celery mixture, sage, and salt.

Drain heart, reserving 1 cup of the cooking liquid; discard bay leaf. Add reserved liquid to corn bread mixture; mix well. Turn stuffing mixture into a 12x7½x2-inch baking dish. Slice heart and place atop stuffing.

Combine mushroom soup and the ¼ cup water; spoon over heart slices. Cover; bake at 350° for 45 minutes. Garnish with parsley sprigs, if desired. Makes 8 servings.

Philadelphia Pepper Pot Soup

2   pounds honeycomb tripe
     Water
     Salt
1   1½-pound veal knuckle
3   medium carrots, sliced
1   large onion, sliced
½   cup sliced celery
2   tablespoons snipped parsley
1   teaspoon salt
1   teaspoon dried marjoram,
      crushed
1   teaspoon dried savory, crushed
1   teaspoon dried basil, crushed
½   teaspoon dried thyme, crushed
½   to 1 teaspoon whole black
      pepper
¼   to ½ teaspoon cayenne
4   whole cloves
2   bay leaves
2   medium potatoes, peeled and
      cut in ½-inch cubes *or* one
      15- or 16-ounce can sliced
      potatoes, drained

Place tripe in Dutch oven; cover with water. Add 1 teaspoon salt for each quart of water used. Simmer, covered, till tripe has clear, jelly-like appearance, 3 to 4 hours. Drain; let tripe stand till cool enough to handle. Cut tripe into ½-inch pieces. Cover and refrigerate.

Meanwhile, in 4-quart Dutch oven place veal knuckle, carrots, onion, celery, parsley, the 1 teaspoon salt, marjoram, savory, basil, thyme, pepper, cayenne, cloves, and bay leaves. Cover with 6 cups water. Simmer, covered, till meat comes off bone, about 2 hours. Strain broth, discarding bones, vegetables, cloves, and bay leaves. Chop meat; return to broth. Cover and refrigerate.

Lift fat from chilled broth. Measure *4 cups* broth; chill remaining. Simmer broth, chopped tripe, and potatoes, covered, till heated through and potatoes are tender, about 15 minutes. Season with salt and pepper. Makes 6 servings.

Crockery cooker directions: Use ingredients as above, *except* use the canned potatoes. Place tripe in electric slow crockery cooker; cover with water. Add 1 teaspoon salt for each quart of water used. Cover; cook on high-heat setting till tripe has clear jelly-like appearance, 6 to 8 hours. (Or, cook on low-heat setting for 16 to 18 hours.) Drain tripe; cover and chill.

In cooker combine carrots, onion, celery, parsley, 1 teaspoon salt, marjoram, savory, basil, thyme, pepper, cayenne, cloves, bay leaves, and 4 cups water. Add veal knuckle. Cover; cook on low-heat setting 10 to 12 hours.

Turn cooker to high-heat setting. Remove meat and vegetables; skim fat from broth. Cut meat from bone; return meat to broth. Discard bone and vegetables.

Cut chilled tripe into ½-inch pieces; stir into broth with *canned* potatoes. Cover; cook on high-heat setting 1 hour. Season to taste with additional salt and pepper. Discard whole cloves and bay leaves.

Tongue and Lima Skillet

1 fresh beef tongue
2 tablespoons chopped onion
1 tablespoon butter *or* margarine
1⅓ cups water
1 10-ounce package frozen baby
    lima beans
1 teaspoon instant beef
    bouillon granules
½ teaspoon Worcestershire sauce
¼ teaspoon dried thyme, crushed
⅓ cup catsup
1 tablespoon cornstarch

Place tongue in saucepan. Cover with salted water. Simmer, covered, allowing 1 hour per pound. Drain tongue; cool. Slit skin on tongue; peel off. Cube enough of the tongue to measure 1½ cups. Refrigerate remaining for sandwiches.

In medium skillet cook onion in butter till tender but not brown. Stir in water, lima beans, instant bouillon granules, Worcestershire, and thyme. Cover and cook according to directions on lima bean package; *do not drain.*

Combine catsup and cornstarch. Stir into bean mixture. Cook and stir till thickened and bubbly. Stir in the 1½ cups cubed cooked tongue; heat through. Makes 4 servings.

Chinese-Style Beef Tongue Pot Roast

1 3-pound fresh beef tongue
1½ cups water
¼ cup soy sauce
1 tablespoon dry sherry
1 clove garlic, minced
2 teaspoons sugar
1 teaspoon salt
¼ teaspoon dried tarragon,
    crushed
¼ teaspoon ground ginger
2¾ cups water
6 medium potatoes, peeled and
    halved
¼ cup cold water
2 tablespoons cornstarch
2 tablespoons sliced green
    onion with tops

In pressure saucepan combine tongue and the 1½ cups water; cook at 15 pounds pressure for 30 minutes. (Or, combine tongue and water in Dutch oven; cook, covered, for 1½ hours.) Drain; cool slightly. Slit skin on tongue and peel off.

In deep bowl combine soy, sherry, garlic, sugar, salt, tarragon, and ginger; add tongue. Marinate 30 minutes at room temperature, turning tongue once.

In large saucepan combine tongue, marinade, and the 2¾ cups water. Cover; simmer 1 hour and 40 minutes. Add potatoes; simmer, covered, till potatoes are tender, 15 to 20 minutes more. Remove tongue and potatoes; keep hot.

Combine the ¼ cup cold water, cornstarch, and onion. Stir into marinade mixture in saucepan. Cook and stir till gravy is thickened and bubbly.

To serve, slice tongue; arrange *half* of the tongue with potatoes on serving platter. (Cover and chill remaining sliced tongue for sandwiches.) Makes 6 servings.

Kidney in Wine Sauce

1 pound beef kidney
1 10½-ounce can condensed beef
    broth
½ cup chopped onion
1 small clove garlic, minced
¼ teaspoon salt
2 carrots, thinly sliced (1 cup)
1 rib celery, sliced (½ cup)
¼ cup dry red wine
2 tablespoons cornstarch
    Hot cooked noodles

Split kidney lengthwise; remove membranes and hard parts. Cut meat in cubes. In saucepan combine meat, condensed broth, onion, garlic, and salt. Cover; simmer for 1½ hours.

Stir in carrot and celery; simmer, covered, till meat and vegetables are tender, about 25 minutes. Blend wine with cornstarch. Stir into meat mixture; cook and stir till thickened and bubbly. Serve over noodles. Serves 4.

Crockery cooker directions: Use ingredients as above. Split kidney lengthwise; remove membranes and hard parts. Cut meat in cubes. In electric slow crockery cooker place meat, condensed beef broth, chopped onion, garlic, salt, thinly sliced carrot, and celery. Cover; cook on low-heat setting for 10 to 12 hours. Turn cooker to high-heat setting; bring mixture to boiling. Blend wine with cornstarch; stir into meat mixture. Cook and stir till thickened. Serve.

Recipes Starring Cooked Beef

Beef Flautas

2 cups thinly sliced cooked beef
    strips (about 12 ounces)
1 tablespoon cooking oil
1 tablespoon red wine vinegar
1½ teaspoons chili powder
½ teaspoon salt
½ teaspoon dried oregano,
    crushed
⅛ teaspoon garlic powder
    Cooking oil
12 corn tortillas
    Avocado Sauce

In skillet brown meat in the 1 tablespoon hot oil; drain. Add red wine vinegar, chili powder, salt, oregano, and garlic powder to meat strips; toss to coat. Set aside.

Pour oil 1 inch deep into 2-quart saucepan; heat. Dip *each* tortilla in hot oil just till soft and limp but not browned, about 5 seconds; drain well on paper toweling.

To assemble flautas, divide beef among tortillas, placing a few strips of meat at one edge of *each* tortilla. Starting at filled edge, roll up tortilla tightly; secure with wooden pick. Fry in hot oil in saucepan till crisp, about 2 minutes. Lift carefully from oil; drain well. Serve with Avocado Sauce. Makes 4 to 6 servings.

Avocado Sauce: Grate enough lemon peel to make ½ teaspoon; set aside. Mash 1 medium ripe avocado (½ cup); stir in 1 teaspoon lemon juice and ¼ teaspoon salt. Blend in ½ cup dairy sour cream; top with lemon peel.

Spicy Blender-Barbecue Beef Sandwiches

2 cups cubed cooked beef
    (about 12 ounces)
1 12-ounce bottle chili sauce
1 8-ounce can tomato sauce
1 thin slice onion
1 small wedge green pepper
1 tablespoon Worcestershire
    sauce
1 teaspoon prepared mustard
¼ teaspoon salt
    Dash bottled hot pepper sauce
10 to 12 hamburger buns, split
    and toasted

Put *half* of the beef in blender container. Cover; blend till chopped. Transfer to saucepan. Repeat with remaining beef. In blender container combine chili sauce, tomato sauce, onion, green pepper, Worcestershire sauce, mustard, salt, and hot pepper sauce; cover and blend till vegetables are chopped. Stir into beef. Simmer, covered, 15 to 20 minutes. Spoon about ¼ cup on each bun. Makes 10 to 12.

Red Flannel Hash

⅓ cup finely chopped onion
2 tablespoons shortening
3 cups finely chopped cooked
    potatoes (3 medium)
1 16-ounce can beets, drained
    and finely chopped
1½ cups finely chopped cooked
    corned beef
⅓ cup milk
½ teaspoon salt
1 or 2 drops bottled hot pepper
    sauce

In skillet cook onion in hot shortening till tender but not brown. Lightly toss together potatoes, beets, corned beef, milk, salt, and hot pepper sauce. Spread hash mixture evenly over onion in skillet.

Cook over medium heat till lightly browned, turning occasionally with spatula. Makes 4 servings.

Make supper a party by serving *Beef Flautas*. Cut last night's cooked beef into strips
and coat with spices; roll in corn tortillas and fry. Then top with an easy-to-make avocado sauce.

Tijuana Sandwiches

3 cups chopped cooked beef
1 16-ounce can refried beans
1 8-ounce can tomato sauce
¾ cup water
½ cup chopped onion
½ cup chopped green pepper
⅓ cup chopped pitted ripe olives
2 teaspoons chili powder
1 teaspoon salt
1 teaspoon Worcestershire
　　sauce
¼ teaspoon garlic powder
¼ teaspoon pepper
¼ teaspoon paprika
　　Dash celery salt
　　Dash ground nutmeg
1 cup crushed corn chips
24 taco shells, heated, *or*
　　hamburger buns,
　　split and toasted
½ medium head lettuce, shredded
2 tomatoes, chopped
1 cup shredded sharp American
　　cheese (4 ounces)
　　Bottled hot pepper sauce

In large skillet or saucepan combine beef, beans, tomato sauce, water, onion, green pepper, olives, chili powder, salt, Worcestershire, garlic powder, pepper, paprika, celery salt, and nutmeg. Simmer, covered, till onion is tender and mixture is hot through, about 20 minutes; stir often.

Just before serving, fold in corn chips. Spoon about ¼ cup mixture into each taco shell; top with a little lettuce, tomato, and cheese. Pass hot pepper sauce. Makes 24.

Crockery cooker directions: Use ingredients as above. In electric slow crockery cooker stir together cooked beef, refried beans, tomato sauce, water, onion, green pepper, and ripe olives. Stir in chili powder, salt, Worcestershire sauce, garlic powder, pepper, paprika, celery salt, and nutmeg. Cover and cook on high-heat setting for 2 hours.

Just before serving, fold in corn chips. Spoon about ¼ *cup* mixture into each taco shell; top with a little lettuce, tomato, and cheese. Pass hot pepper sauce.

Pepperoni-Beef Spaghetti Sauce

1 28-ounce can tomatoes
1 6-ounce can tomato paste
1 medium green pepper, cut up
1 small onion, cut up
1 clove garlic
2 teaspoons sugar
1 teaspoon salt
½ teaspoon dried oregano,
　　crushed
½ teaspoon dried basil, crushed
½ teaspoon chili powder
⅛ teaspoon pepper
2 cups finely chopped or
　　coarsely ground
　　cooked beef
1 4-ounce package sliced
　　pepperoni, finely chopped
　　or coarsely ground
　　(about 1 cup)
　　Hot cooked spaghetti
　　Grated Parmesan cheese

In blender container combine undrained tomatoes, tomato paste, green pepper, onion, garlic, sugar, salt, oregano, basil, chili powder, and pepper. Cover and blend just till vegetables are chopped.

Pour sauce mixture into a 3-quart saucepan. Add beef and pepperoni. Bring to boiling; reduce heat. Simmer, uncovered, for 15 minutes. Serve sauce over hot spaghetti; pass Parmesan cheese. Makes 6 servings.

Crockery cooker directions: Prepare sauce mixture in blender container as above. Pour sauce in electric slow crockery cooker. Add beef and pepperoni. Cover; cook on high-heat setting for 3 to 3½ hours. Serve over spaghetti; pass Parmesan.

Adapted from an Indian classic, *Beef Curry* is made with leftover beef and served over rice. Accompany it with condiments, such as chutney, coconut, bacon, bananas, and peanuts.

Beef Curry

½ **cup chopped onion**
2 **teaspoons curry powder**
1 **tablespoon cooking oil**
2 **cups cubed cooked beef**
   (about 12 ounces)
2 **small apples, peeled and**
   sliced or chopped (1 cup)
¾ **cup water**
½ **cup raisins**
1 **teaspoon instant beef bouillon**
   granules
½ **teaspoon salt**
¼ **cup cold water**
1 **tablespoon all-purpose flour**
   Hot cooked rice
   Condiments (optional)

In 10-inch skillet cook onion and curry powder in hot oil till onion is tender. Stir in cubed beef, sliced or chopped apples, the ¾ cup water, raisins, instant beef bouillon granules, and salt. Cover and simmer for 10 minutes.

Blend the ¼ cup cold water with flour; stir into skillet mixture. Cook and stir till thickened and bubbly. Season to taste with additional salt and pepper. Serve over hot cooked rice. If desired, pass condiments, such as crumbled cooked bacon, shredded coconut, chutney, peanuts, and sliced bananas. Makes 4 or 5 servings.

Pepper Steak Salad

3 cups rare-cooked roast beef
    cut in thin strips
    (about 1 pound)
2 small tomatoes, cut in wedges
1 large green pepper, cut in
    strips
1 cup sliced celery
⅓ cup sliced green onion with
    tops
⅓ cup sliced fresh mushrooms
½ cup teriyaki sauce
⅓ cup dry sherry
⅓ cup salad oil
3 tablespoons white *or* rice
    vinegar
½ teaspoon ground ginger
1 cup fresh *or* canned bean
    sprouts, rinsed
4 cups shredded Chinese cabbage

In bowl combine beef strips, tomato wedges, green pepper, celery, green onion, and fresh mushrooms. In screw-top jar combine teriyaki sauce, dry sherry, salad oil, vinegar, and ginger; shake well. Pour over beef mixture; toss to coat well. Cover and refrigerate 2 to 3 hours.

Add bean sprouts to beef mixture; toss again. Drain, reserving marinade. Place shredded cabbage in large salad bowl; top with marinated meat and vegetable mixture. Pass reserved marinade for dressing. Makes 6 servings,

Frenchy Beef Salad

3 cups cubed cooked potatoes
¼ cup French salad dressing
1½ cups cubed cooked beef
1 cup sliced celery
½ cup sliced radishes
½ cup mayonnaise *or* salad
    dressing
⅓ cup chili sauce
¼ cup dairy sour cream
2 tablespoons sliced green onion
    with tops
1 tablespoon lemon juice
½ teaspoon salt
    Lettuce cups

In bowl combine potatoes and French dressing. In another bowl stir together beef, celery, radishes, mayonnaise, chili sauce, sour cream, green onion, lemon juice, and salt. Stir beef mixture into potatoes; cover and chill. Serve in lettuce cups. Makes 6 servings.

Beef Supper Salad

⅓ cup mayonnaise *or* salad
    dressing
¼ cup chili sauce
1 tablespoon sweet pickle relish
½ teaspoon salt
1 8-ounce can red kidney beans
2 cups cubed cooked beef
1 cup sliced celery
½ cup chopped onion
2 hard-cooked eggs, chopped

Blend together mayonnaise, chili sauce, sweet pickle relish, salt, and dash pepper. Drain kidney beans; combine beans, beef, celery, onion, and eggs. Add dressing mixture; toss lightly. Cover and refrigerate up to 24 hours. Stir salad before serving. Makes 4 or 5 servings.

A tangy horseradish dressing coats *Peachy Beef Toss*. Sure to be a summertime hit, this main dish salad uses leftover roast beef, greens, fresh peaches, tomatoes, and avocado.

Peachy Beef Toss

    1 **head romaine, torn in bite-**
      size pieces (4 cups)
    3 **cups fresh spinach torn in**
      bite-size pieces
 1½ **cups cooked roast beef cut**
      in strips
    3 **fresh medium peaches, peeled,**
      pitted, and sliced (1½ cups)
    1 **medium ripe avocado, peeled,**
      pitted, and sliced
   12 **cherry tomatoes, halved**
   ½ **cup salad oil**
    3 **tablespoons vinegar**
    1 **tablespoon prepared**
      horseradish
   ½ **teaspoon salt**
   ½ **teaspoon Worcestershire**
      sauce
   ⅛ **teaspoon pepper**
    2 **drops bottled hot pepper**
      sauce

In salad bowl combine romaine, spinach, cooked roast beef, sliced peaches, sliced avocado, and cherry tomato halves.

In screw-top jar combine salad oil, vinegar, horseradish, salt, Worcestershire sauce, pepper, and hot pepper sauce. Cover and shake well.

Just before serving, pour dressing mixture over salad; toss lightly. Makes 6 servings.

Bamboula

½ pound ground pork
1 cup finely chopped celery
¾ cup water
¼ cup chopped onion
1 teaspoon instant beef
    bouillon granules
1 cup milk
¼ cup all-purpose flour
2 tablespoons snipped parsley
2 tablespoons sliced pitted
    ripe olives
1 tablespoon catsup
¾ teaspoon salt
¼ teaspoon pepper
2 recipes Plain Pastry
    (see below)
1½ cups chopped cooked beef

Brown the pork; drain. Set aside. In saucepan combine celery, water, onion, and bouillon granules. Cover; simmer 10 minutes. Do not drain. Blend milk with flour; stir into celery mixture. Cook and stir till slightly thickened and bubbly. Stir in pork, parsley, olives, catsup, salt, and pepper. Bring to boiling; set aside.

Prepare Plain Pastry as for a double-crust pie. Spoon chopped beef on bottom crust; top with hot pork mixture. Adjust top crust; seal. Cut slits in top for escape of steam. Fold foil strip around pastry rim to avoid overbrowning. Bake at 400° till golden brown, 30 to 35 minutes. Let stand 15 minutes before serving. Makes 6 servings.

One-Crust Frozen Pot Pies

½ cup finely chopped celery
½ cup finely chopped onion
¼ cup snipped parsley
3 tablespoons butter *or*
    margarine
3 tablespoons all-purpose flour
¼ teaspoon salt
⅛ teaspoon pepper
3 cups beef broth
2 cups diced cooked beef
½ cup cooked peas
½ cup diced cooked carrots
    Plain Pastry (see below)

In saucepan cook celery, onion, and parsley in butter till tender. Blend in flour, salt, and pepper; add broth all at once. Cook and stir till thickened and bubbly; stir in meat, peas, and carrots. Cover; chill thoroughly.

Divide chilled meat mixture evenly among six 4½x1-inch pie plates. Prepare Plain Pastry; divide into 6 equal portions. Roll each to a 5-inch circle. Place one circle atop each pie; seal to edge of dish. Wrap pies separately in heavy foil; seal, label, and freeze.

To serve, unwrap and cut slits in top crust. Place on baking sheet; do not thaw. Bake frozen pies at 425° till golden, about 40 minutes. Cover edges with foil the last 10 minutes, if necessary, to prevent overbrowning. (Bake unfrozen pies 20 to 25 minutes.) Makes 6 servings.

Plain Pastry (enough for one 9-inch pie crust)

1 cup all-purpose flour
½ teaspoon salt
⅓ cup shortening
3 to 4 tablespoons cold water

Stir together flour and salt; cut in shortening till pieces are the size of small peas. Sprinkle *1 tablespoon* water over part of the mixture. Gently toss with fork; push to side of bowl. Repeat till all is moistened. Form dough into a ball. Continue as directed in recipe.

For single-crust pie: Flatten dough on lightly floured surface. Roll from center to edge till ⅛ inch thick. Fit pastry circle into a 9-inch pie plate. Trim ½ to 1 inch beyond edge of pie plate. Fold under and flute edge. Continue as directed in recipe.

For double-crust pie: Prepare dough as directed above *except* double the recipe. Form into two balls. Flatten each ball on a lightly floured surface. Roll each from center to edge till ⅛ inch thick. Fit one pastry circle into a 9-inch pie plate. Trim crust even with rim of plate. Continue as directed in recipe, sealing and fluting top crust..

Index

Q-R

S

Storm Across Asia

Genghis Khan and the Mongols

The Mogul Expansion

Empires

Their Rise and Fall

Storm
Across Asia

Genghis Khan and the Mongols

The Mogul Expansion

Henry Wiencek
Genghis Khan and the Mongols

**Glenn D. Lowry
with Amanda Heller**
The Mogul Expansion

Preface by W. M. Thackston, Jr.
Senior Preceptor in Persian
Harvard University

Boston Publishing Company, Inc.
Boston, Massachusetts

Empires: Their Rise and Fall is published in the United States by Boston Publishing Company, Inc., and distributed by Field Publications.

Authors: Henry Wiencek, Glenn D. Lowry, Amanda Heller
Picture Researcher, Janet Adams
Assistant Picture Researcher, Lynn Bowdery
Historical Consultant, Kenneth Maxwell
Project Consultant, Valerie Hopkins
Design Implementation, Designworks

Boston Publishing Company, Inc.

President, Robert J. George
Editor-In-Chief, Robert Manning
Managing Editor, Paul Dreyfus
Marketing Director, Jeanne Gibson

Field Publications

President, Bruce H. Seide
Publisher, Marilyn Black
Marketing Director, Kathleen E. Long

Rizzoli Editore

Authors of the Italian Edition
   Introduction: Professor Ovidio Dallera
   Genghis Khan and the Mongols: Drs. Ada and Alberto
     Vacchi
   The Mogul Expansion: Dr. Sergio Stocchi
   Maps: Gian Franco Leonardi
Idea and Realization, Harry C. Lindinger
Graphic Design, Gerry Valsecchi
General Editorial Supervisor, Ovidio Dallera

© 1986 by Rizzoli Editore
Printed in United States.

Library of Congress Catalog Card Number: 79-2519
ISBN: 0-15-004029-6

Contents

Preface

Before the age of discovery and global awareness, contacts between Europeans and the peoples of central Asia and the Indian subcontinent were few and isolated. Two of the peoples in this vast region to leave a lasting mark on Western consciousness are the Mongols and the Moguls. Both of these names still conjure vivid images in the mind. The Mongols evoke dread and fear—Slavs still pray in their litanies that God will preserve them from the "wrath of the Tatar"—and the Moguls of India, distant kindred of the Mongols, have lent their name to autocratic potentates and to anything grandiose or lavish. Both peoples founded empires by force of conquest and long after assimilation to their subject peoples in most facets of life maintained institutions derived from the nomadic traditions of the central Asian steppe, such as land tenure based on military patronage and a preference for highly mobile courts over fixed capital cities.

In the first half of the thirteenth century, mention of the Mongol hordes—the "Scourge of God"—could cause trepidation from the Atlantic to the Pacific. Some attempted valiantly but vainly to resist the Mongols, while others resigned themselves to their doom at the hands of what were considered instruments of God's punishment for the sins of mankind. Those who experienced firsthand the wrath of the invading armies indeed had cause for alarm. Having relatively few fighting men for an all-conquering army and lacking the experience and will to administer vast regions of settled peoples, the Mongols elected to destroy as a matter of course what was not perceived by them to be of immediate benefit. Only after the breakup of the unified empire of Genghis Khan and his sons did the Mongols begin to see the advantage of proper administration.

Although the cultural level of the Mongols themselves was abysmally low in comparison to that of the Chinese and Persians they conquered, all the havoc and destruction wrought by the "apes of saddles" (to quote an Arab poet of Baghdad) did not bring civilization to a halt, as had been predicted; in fact, an unprecedented cultural flowering took place in Mongol-governed China and Iran. Under the patronage of Mongol rulers, who were rapidly assimilated into the cultural milieu of their subject peoples, artists created what became classic norms of literature, painting, and architecture. The concurrent resurgence of interest in mysticism in both Europe and the Islamic world during the thirteenth century may have had its nascence in a turning inward to escape the all-too-real physical threat of the Mongols. In the economic prosperity and social revival that followed, mysticism and mystically tinged literature continued to flourish, especially in the Iranian world.

Quite different from the devastating onslaught of the Mongols was the arrival of the Moguls in India. Zahir ud-Din Mohammed Baber, a descendant of Genghis Khan, brought his followers from their ancestral home of Transoxiana in central Asia into the Indus Valley, where they found a Moslem ruling elite that had adopted many of their cultural notions wholesale from the Persianate literary culture of Iran—as the Moguls themselves had done. Baber and his son Humayun initially represented little more than two in a long series of foreign rulers from the north who had successively assumed a tenuous control over northern India. Under Akbar and his successors, though, the empire expanded to include the greater part of the subcontinent, in part because of a shrewd alliance with the militant Rajput warrior-princes.

More important, the dominant Persianizing cultural modes, fed by a constant influx of talent from Safawid Iran, were synthesized with native Indian elements during the Mogul period to create a vibrant grace and refinement bolstered by practically limitless wealth. Under Mogul patronage, the arts attained a technical perfection that was uniquely Mogul in style and conceptualization and rarely rivaled in all of Islamic civilization. Unfortunately, the empire was unable to create a society as integrated as its arts or to deal successfully with the tensions it had created, and it soon crumbled politically; the pieces were subsequently gathered by the British and incorporated into their Indian Empire. Still, the legacy that the Moguls bequeathed to India in literature, music, architecture, and painting remains one of the most notable achievements of world civilization.

W. M. THACKSTON, JR.
Senior Preceptor in Persian
Harvard University

Genghis Khan and the Mongols

In the winter of 1206, the treasurers of the emperor of North China reported that one of the empire's less important vassals, the Mongol khan, had neglected to pay the annual tribute required of a loyal subject. A prince was dispatched to find the camp of the Mongols—somewhere in "the distant land" north of the Gobi Desert—and collect the payment, but there was little anxiety at the Peking court. The Chinese had defeated Mongol bands before and had managed to keep them in a state of powerless disunity. Indeed, the Mongols were despised by other nomadic tribes for their poverty and ignorance: They had no wealth aside from their horses and sheep, made nothing worth trading with foreigners, and, unlike their more

Preceding page, a yurt, or Mongol tent. Made of felt stretched over a frame of wooden slats, the yurt of today differs little from that of Genghis Khan's time—eight hundred years ago—when it was the only means of shelter for the nomadic Mongols.

Above, a landscape in Mongolia. High mountain ranges—the Altai and the Khangai—alternating with steppe that averages over 5,200 feet in altitude shield much of the terrain. Some mountain peaks soar to 13,000 feet above sea level. Lake Baikal (right), which formed a part of the Mongol realm, is now under Soviet control.

tribesmen had been achieved only after two decades of wars waged by Genghis Khan to bring under his sway "all the people who dwell in felt tents." Genghis Khan assembled the tribes in 1206 so that he could publicly proclaim a nation called "The Blue Mongols," under the protection of the heavenly sky. Before the gathering of princes he recounted the deeds of his warriors, praised those who had been loyal to him, promulgated a system of laws by which he would govern, and selected a "bodyguard"—an army

civilized Turkish neighbors, could not read or write.

As the Chinese prince was making his way north, he was surprised to encounter Turks and Mongols from as far east as the Khingan Mountains and as far west as the Altai Mountains also heading for the khan's headquarters. His apprehension grew when he reached the camp and saw the tent of the chief, Genghis Khan, decorated with fine brocades and gold plaques. The khan handed over the usual gifts and hurried the prince on his way back to Peking. Once in Peking, the prince's warnings about the new wealth and power of the Mongols were dismissed. The emperor felt secure behind the thirteen-hundred-year-old Great Wall, and his chief commander asserted that all was quiet among the roaming tribesmen of the north.

The calm that prevailed among the northern

Above, part of a herd of cattle in Mongolia today. The descendants of Genghis Khan make their living largely from herding, as did their ancestors centuries ago.

Above right, a scene in Mongolia, showing in the background the yurts used for shelter on the steppe. Right, a steppe landscape.

of ten thousand men. Privately, he revealed his intention of invading China, not on a hasty raid for plunder but on a prolonged expedition of conquest.

Genghis Khan did not then foresee that he would set in motion a machine of conquest that would establish the largest empire in history. In the next century, Mongol warriors would invade Japan, come within sixty miles of Venice, impose their rule from Korea to Hungary, found a new dynasty in China, and create a regime in Russia that was to last over two hundred years. The Mongol Empire is remarkable for the speed of its conquest, and most of all for its size, and most unlikely creators—a confederation of

nomads from one of the most forbidding places on earth.

The homeland of the Mongols lay along the banks of the Onon River, a branch of the Amur that today forms part of the border between China and the Soviet Union. The Onon basin is rich grassland, part of the steppe that stretches from Manchuria all the way to Hungary, interrupted but not entirely blocked by the Altai Mountains of central Asia. To the south and west of the Altai are the Pamirs, the Hindu Kush, and the Himalayas, towering mountain ranges that cut off East Asia from Middle Asia. The steppe lands

These pages, some of the lands over which the Mongols of Genghis Khan held sway. Left, an Afghan valley near Bamian, a city destroyed by Genghis Khan in 1220. Above, the landscape of Georgia—now a Soviet republic between the Caucasus Mountains and Turkey—where the Mongol invasion of Europe began. Right, a river valley in Azerbaijan, Iran, a region that was a stronghold of the Mongol rule in Persia. Following pages, a view of a forbidding desert in Afghanistan, one of the natural barriers crossed by the Mongols.

where the Mongols first lived are separated from China by the Gobi Desert, where lakes and rivers have been known to dry up before the eyes of travelers and sand dunes to shift in the course of a night. Because all landmarks might disappear before daybreak, local caravan guides would lay out arrows pointing the right direction of travel before nightfall. The steppe itself is only slightly more hospitable than the desert. Temperatures range from forty degrees below freezing in winter to over one hundred in summer—and even then bitter winds from Siberia blow down with incredible suddenness. (A European missionary who journeyed to the Mongol court in the thirteenth century wrote that the wind could almost blow a rider off his horse, and he described a hailstorm so heavy that men were drowned when the hail melted.)

The Mongols and Turks who inhabited the steppe endured a rough life as herders of sheep and cattle and breeders of horses. They were also proficient hunters but regarded hunting more as sport and training for war than as a livelihood. In fact they were contemptuous of the hunters of the Siberian forest, though their opinion of city dwellers was even lower. The Mongols moved with the seasons in search of pastures, living in tents known as yurts. The yurt was

The forerunners of the Mongols

Some six centuries before the Mongols established their empire, another people of the Asian steppe—the Turks—created a realm stretching from Mongolia to the Black Sea. This was only the first of the Turkish empires, which had a far more lasting impact on history than the Mongol Empire. (The last Turkish empire, the Ottoman, lasted until World War One.)

In the tenth century, Turkish mercenaries in the service of the Persians overthrew their masters and established the short-lived Ghaznavid Empire, which was supplanted in the eleventh century by the Seljuk Empire. (The pictures on these pages depict some of the battles of this period.) By 1055, Seljuk armies had conquered territory as far west as Baghdad, and sixteen years later they defeated the Byzantine emperor at Manzikert, winning the region now known as Turkey. The Seljuk realm, which extended from what is now western China to the Mediterranean, broke up in the twelfth century, with the regions of Persia and Khwarizm conquered by Mohammed II. This monarch provoked Genghis Khan by murdering a Mongol ambassador and lost his realm in the subsequent war of revenge.

A large part of Genghis Khan's army was composed of Turks. Because the Turks were literate and more civilized than the Mongols, they played an important part in the government of the Mongol Empire.

This page, top and bottom, Turkish troops battling each other in Khorasan early in the eleventh century, when rival factions struggled for power. The drum in the top picture was used to pace horses at the beginning of an attack. Immediately above, a Turkish general and a scribe.

Below, a cavalry battle between Turkish factions. Above and left, the siege of the fortress of Arg, near Bukhara, in 1003. The catapult in the left picture is similar to the one later used by the Mongols.

made of felt and was usually supported by wooden rods that could be taken apart quickly and packed onto wagons. (Only the chief of a tribe had a permanent tent, which could be moved intact on an enormous wagon.)

Because the Mongols lived at the mercy of their surroundings, it is not surprising that their religious practices reveal a deep respect for nature. The Mongols venerated the sky, the moon, and the stars, and they genuflected before the sun at dawn. Rivers were sacred, and the Mongols took elaborate precautions to avoid polluting them; washing or urinating in a stream, for example, was forbidden. The Mongols also revered fire as a purifying element; trash was never burned, nor could a knife be passed through a fire lest it "behead" the flames.

Below, Genghis Khan in front of a tent with some of his retainers. Born around 1167, Genghis Khan was given the name Temujin, after a Tatar chieftain his father had captured in battle. At the age of twenty-eight, Temujin was elected khan, or chief, of the Mongols and received the title Genghis ("Universal").

In every yurt there were several idols representing gods that watched over the occupants. At every meal the Mongols fed each god by rubbing meat and broth over the mouths of the idols. In number the gods were virtually infinite, signifying a universal supernatural presence. When a Moslem imam described his faith to Genghis Khan, the Mongol leader asked: "Why do you make the pilgrimage to Mecca? Do you not know that god is everywhere?"

The priests of the Mongol religion—shamans—held

Above, a portrait of Yesugai, the father of Genghis Khan. Yesugai was a prominent figure in the Mongols' wars against the Chin emperors of North China and their allies in the decades before Temujin's birth. Even after the Chinese and their allies smashed a confederation of Mongols, Yesugai was able to retain the loyalty of a few tribes until his death. Below, a Persian depiction of Mongol cavalry in action. The Mongols always fought on horseback, using bows and arrows, swords, and lances as their main weapons.

19

Left, the Mongol army besieging a Persian town. During Genghis Khan's wars in the Middle East, millions of soldiers and civilians were killed; many towns and farming areas did not recover from the devastation for decades. Top, the Mongol army facing an enemy force across a river on the steppe. Immediately above, a surprise attack on a camp.

a position of great honor in society. They communed with the gods and the spirits of the dead, going into trances and ecstasies during visits to heaven or the underworld. Accounts have survived of the complex rituals acted out by shamans to purify a tent after someone had died there. In the presence of the dead person's relatives the shaman entered a trance, spoke in the voice of the dead, and conducted the deceased's spirit to the underworld. Before any important undertaking the khan consulted a shaman, who would then speak with the gods and communicate their commands to the khan. The religious powers of the shamans gave them great secular authority, which Genghis Khan himself was forced to deal with head on. Once, when the chief shaman spread rumors alleging the disloyalty of the khan's brother, Genghis Khan allowed the shaman to be killed—a calculated act of sacrilege that terrified the people and symbolized Genghis Khan's absolute power.

After their conquests, the Mongols adopted the religions of their subjects—mainly Islam and Buddhism—and did not persecute any faith. The Mongols had a lively interest in the beliefs of foreigners and recognized the political advantages of religious tolerance, which was decreed by Genghis Khan's law. Visitors to the Mongol capital of Karakorum were struck by the presence of mosques, churches, and temples alongside one another.

Much of what is known about the Mongols derives from accounts written by Europeans who visited the Mongol Empire, notably Marco Polo, Giovanni de Piano Carpini, and William of Rubruck. The only Mongol sources are a history written in the seventeenth century by a man who claimed descent from Genghis Khan, and *The Secret History of the Mongols,* a thirteenth-century text that combines history with legend. In the fashion of the *Iliad* and the *Odyssey, The Secret History* chronicles the heroic exploits of Genghis Khan that were originally told around smoky dung fires in the Mongol yurts.

The legendary deeds recounted in the *The Secret History* inflamed the imagination and pride of the Mongols, convincing them that Genghis Khan was heaven-sent to unite the nomads against their enemies. Even Genghis Khan's birth, around 1167, was portentous: According to the chronicle, the future conquerer came into the world prophetically clutching a clot of black blood. His father named him Temujin, after an enemy chief he had captured in battle. As a teenager, Temujin was already a famous figure among the Mongols, reputed to have hunted down a band of thieves with only one companion and retrieved his family's stolen horses in a running battle with bow and arrow. The Mongols marveled at tales of how the youth escaped from an enemy camp with his neck locked in a wooden stock. It was even said that heaven directed a falcon to feed Temujin when

Left, stone monoliths—believed to date from the time of Genghis Khan—about one hundred miles from Ulan Bator, the capital of modern Mongolia. Below, a votive stele engraved with the name of Genghis Khan. After his death, Genghis Khan was literally idolized by many Mongols. Images of the khan were placed in tents, and foreigners who refused to pay homage to the idols were killed.

he was hiding from pursuers and that a giant rock fell into his path from nowhere when he was about to ride into an ambush.

Before he was thirty, Temujin's prowess in battle, his generosity in sharing spoils, and his shrewd diplomacy won him tens of thousands of followers. The Mongol princes chose him to be their khan, or ruler, and bestowed on him the name Genghis ("Universal"). Nonetheless, opponents of Genghis Khan's rule were numerous, and years of tribal warfare followed the election. All adversaries were subdued or dead by 1206, the year that marks the beginning of the Mongol Empire.

In 1207 a delegation from Peking again made its way to the Onon to inform Genghis Khan that a new emperor had ascended the throne of China—the prince of Wei. On hearing this, Genghis Khan stated that the emperor "must be an eminent personage, designated by heaven." He then asked: "How can an imbecile like the prince of Wei perform such a role?" Before the astonished ambassadors could make any response, the khan spat contemptuously and rode off.

The enmity between the nomads of the steppe and the farmers and traders of China dated as far back as the third century B.C., when the Chinese began to build the Great Wall along their border to keep out

These stone remains (above, in the fore-ground) in Soviet Kazakhstan are believed by some to date from the Mongol era. Right, a stone lion from the Mongols' capital of Karakorum.

raiding parties. In the tenth century, barbarians from the north known as the Khitan conquered much of North China, including Peking. The Chinese Sung emperors, forced to retreat to South China, sought the help of Juchen nomads. The Juchen ousted the Khitan but then—to the great surprise of the Sung—set themselves up as the Chin ("Golden") emperors. This was the situation in China when Genghis Khan began his invasion in 1211.

For two years the Mongol army, accustomed to battles fought on horseback in the open, was blocked by the Great Wall and had to content itself with taking border outposts. The breakthrough finally

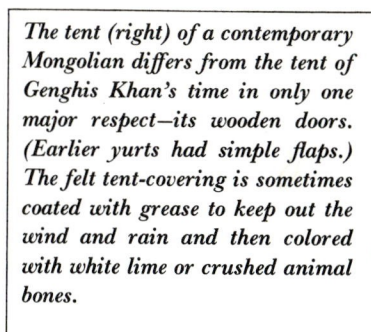

The tent (right) of a contemporary Mongolian differs from the tent of Genghis Khan's time in only one major respect—its wooden doors. (Earlier yurts had simple flaps.) The felt tent-covering is sometimes coated with grease to keep out the wind and rain and then colored with white lime or crushed animal bones.

Below, the interior of a modern yurt. The wooden strips that support the tent can be quickly disassembled and stacked for transport. The opening at the top permits smoke from the cooking fire to escape.

The Mongols' simple shelters

The Mongols' nomadic way of life necessitated a shelter that was easily taken apart and transported but yet sturdy enough to withstand the high winds and extreme temperatures of the steppes. The yurt met all these requirements admirably: Its wooden framework was collapsible, its felt walls could be rolled up, and the entire structure could be transported handily on horses or oxen.

The Mongols had no desire to live in permanent buildings, and even after amassing great wealth through their conquests they continued to use yurts as their homes. The tents' furnishings were simple: a bed with a rough woolen mattress, animal skins for blankets, and wicker baskets lined with felt to serve as clothes chests. At the center of the yurt was the fire used for cooking; it was placed under a hole in the roof to allow the smoke to escape.

The traditional yurt has survived in Mongolia to the present day.

Above and left, two views of the sumptuously decorated yurts used by Mongol nobles in Genghis Khan's time. Below, a Mongolian woman and boy standing in front of a yurt. The boy's cap is remarkably similar to the one worn by ancient Mongol warriors.

In the winter of 1220, during the war against Khwarizm, Genghis Khan captured the city of Bukhara. The inhabitants surrendered and were not mistreated, though the khan did order that an enormous ransom be paid immediately in exchange for their safety. Immediately below, the ransom demand being made. Bottom, the walls of the citadel of Bukhara, where a garrison held out after the citizens of the city had capitulated. In storming the garrison, the Mongols inadvertently started fires that leveled the city. Near right, the minaret of a mosque in Bukhara.

Top right, a mausoleum built in Bukhara in the fourteenth century, when the city was reconstructed by Moslem governors installed by the Mongols. Center right, Genghis Khan haranguing the citizens of Bukhara after his victory, claiming that he represents the punishment of God for their rulers' misdeeds.

came when Genghis Khan ordered Jebe, one of his generals, to head a detachment of riders into a seventeen-mile-long gorge that led to the plain beyond the wall. Jebe charged the Chin defenders of the gorge but then suddenly retreated, luring the Chin defenders out of their positions. With the Chin troops in headlong pursuit, Jebe's shocked troops turned and charged again. At that moment, Genghis Khan appeared behind Jebe, and the Mongols routed the Chin.

This decisive victory unleashed the Mongol horde into the plains of China, where they trampled fields and pillaged towns for two years. In 1215 a Chin general went over to the Mongols and led them into Peking. At this point, Genghis Khan placed a general in charge of a series of sieges. The khan then returned to Mongolia so that he might better attend to a pressing matter in the west.

The son of one of Genghis Khan's tribal enemies had taken refuge among the Kara-Khitan, whose kingdom was in the steppe south of Lake Balkhash (now in the south-central Soviet Union). The exiled Mongol had treacherously imprisoned the king of the Kara-Khitan, placed himself on the throne, and begun oppressing the people, particularly his Moslem subjects. When the Kara-Khitan appealed for aid,

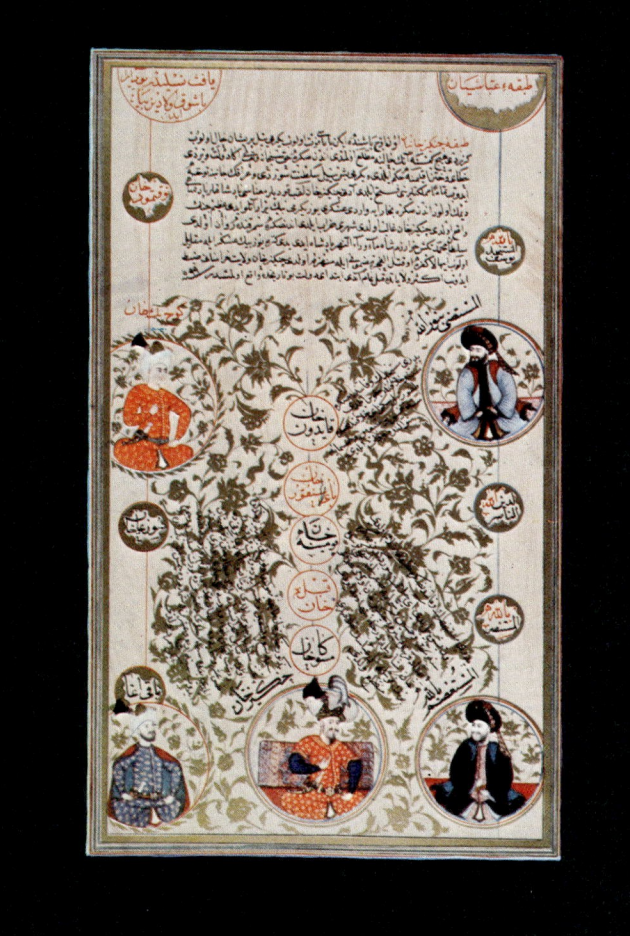

This page, three representations of Genghis Khan. Above, a fourteenth-century Persian view of a court scene. The khan here wears a long-sleeved robe so that supplicants will not actually touch him. Left, a manuscript leaf, with the khan the center figure at the bottom of the page. Below, a Chinese artist's portrait of Genghis Khan hunting with a falcon.

Above, a thirteenth-century Persian cup with a representation of a Mongol horseman. Right, the elevation of Temujin to Genghis Khan, as depicted in a Persian miniature.

Genghis Khan sent his trusted general Jebe, who was immediately welcomed as a savior. The gates of the capital were thrown open to Jebe, and the Kara-Khitan hunted down the supporters of the usurpers. By restraining his men from pillage and by authorizing the free practice of all religions, Jebe ingratiated himself with the local inhabitants, who gladly placed themselves under the banner of Genghis Khan.

Acquisition of the lands of the Kara-Khitan brought the Mongols in contact for the first time with the highly developed Moslem civilization of the Persians and Arabs. From the Hindu Kush to the Persian Gulf and the Caspian Sea stretched the empire of Khwarizm, one of the oldest centers of Asian civilization. Its capital, Urgench, was a seat of Moslem learning, and Samarkand was a city fabled throughout Asia for its lush gardens fed by skillfully built canals in the middle of a desert. Metals, leather, and cloth from Samarkand were prized luxuries, and the wealthy purchased Samarkand melons transported in lead casks filled with snow.

The merchants and rulers of this wealthy empire, including Shah Mohammed II, regarded the Mongols as ignorant barbarians who could easily be exploited. Khwarizmian merchants led a caravan to the encampment of Genghis Khan and brazenly over-charged him for everything he bought. To show that he had caught on to them, the khan confiscated the entire caravan—but then made amends by paying the traders even more than they had expected. The khan had an ambassador accompany the traders on their return to Khwarizm, instructing him to inform the shah: "I have the greatest desire to live in peace with you. I shall look on you as my son. . . . You know that my country is an ant heap of warriors, a mine of silver, and that I have no need to covet other dominions. We have an equal interest in fostering trade between our subjects."

To demonstrate his intentions, Genghis Khan dispatched a caravan with samples of the riches of his empire: a train of five hundred camels bearing precious metals, silk from China, and furs. In addition, the princes of the Mongol Empire each sent a personal buyer to acquire Khwarizmian goods. When the caravan reached the frontier, though, one of the shah's governors seized all the goods and put the Mongols to death. Genghis Khan, enraged, dispatched an ambassador to demand that the governor be handed over for a Mongol trial. The shah then executed the ambassador—an act the Mongols regarded as an unforgiveable atrocity, one that could be rectified only by war.

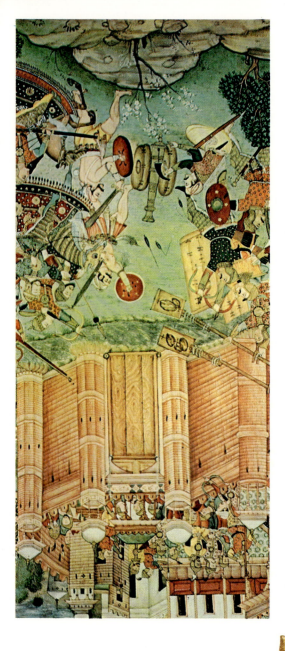

The Mongols' war against China, launched in 1211, continued intermittently for over sixty years. Below, Mongol and Chinese cavalry fighting a battle in a mountain pass. Above right, Mongol engineers diverting a Chinese river—a tactic also used by the Mongols in their Middle Eastern wars.

Below, a Persian depiction of the Mongols besieging a Chinese city. Historians consider it unlikely, however, that the Mongols used cannons in the Chinese wars. Right, the Great Wall of China, which delayed the Mongol invasion for two years.

The Mongol horde that set out for the empire of Khwarizm in 1219 was a disciplined, well-drilled force, and its generals were without equals in any nation. (Though the word "horde" suggests a disorganized rabble, its root word in the Mongol language—*orda*—simply means "a camp.") Genghis Khan divided the army into decimal units. The smallest was a group of ten, and the largest a ten-thousand-man outfit. The basic weapon of every Mongol soldier was the bow and arrow, which had a range of perhaps three hundred yards. The entire army was provided with horses, and every soldier was assured a fresh mount during battle. When Mongol command-

ers needed infantry to bear the brunt of an assault against a heavily defended bastion, they drove prisoners and civilians in front of the ranks of horsemen. Captives were also forced to fill in trenches with dirt and position siege equipment under fire.

The army's battle line was five men deep. The front two ranks were heavy cavalry—men armed with lances and wearing chest armor made of hide or pieces of iron sewn into leather. Behind them were three ranks of light cavalry wearing light leather armor. Every soldier wore a shirt of raw silk as protection against arrow wounds. An arrow would push the silk into the wound ahead of it so that a field

doctor (the army was attended by Chinese and, later, Persian physicians) could dislodge the arrow by simply removing the fabric.

The Mongol's favorite tactic in a pitched battle was to send a "suicide corps" galloping toward the enemy ranks. The corps would then turn and fake a retreat to tempt the enemy into a disorganized chase. When the enemy was strung out in pursuit and their horses tired, the entire Mongol force would charge into them according to a set plan. The light cavalry would gallop back and forth pelting the enemy with arrows, after which the heavy cavalry charged in with their lances. The field commanders directed these

Genghis Khan's war against Khwarizm was a whirlwind of destruction and slaughter. Above and left, the ruins of Bamian, a city in what is now Afghanistan. A center of Buddhism, where more than one thousand monks lived in monasteries, the city fiercely resisted a Mongol siege in 1221. Genghis Khan eventually took personal control of the siege and leveled the city, which remained uninhabited for forty years. So great was the devastation that Bamian was renamed the "accursed place."

Genghis Khan and the Mongols

Modern scholars have called his strategy for the Khwarizmian campaign one of the most brilliant in military history.

Trusting to surprise and mobility to make the difference, Subotai split the badly outnumbered Mongol forces into four armies—a southern arm, two central thrusts, and a northern flanking force. As the southern wing entered Khwarizm and engaged the shah's forces, the two center groups attacked the cities of Khojend and Otrar. Khojend fell quickly to the Mongol attackers. The defenders of Otrar, the seat of the governor who had touched off the war by slaughtering the Mongol caravan, fought fiercely, realizing they would receive no quarter. The siege of the city lasted five months, and at its end only the governor, his wife, and a few guards remained alive. The few survivors took refuge on a roof and hurled tiles on the attackers when their arrows ran out. The Mongols burrowed into the building until it collapsed and pulled the governor alive out of the rubble. As fitting punishment for his greed, the governor was put to

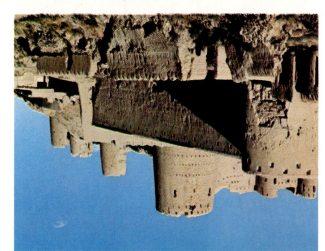

Genghis Khan and the Mongols Center, above and below, the ruins of Bamian. Near left, Herat, another city in present-day Afghanistan razed by order of Genghis Khan after all its inhabitants had been slain in a week-long slaughter. Below, a battle in Khwarizm as recorded by a Persian artist.

Preceding pages, the funeral procession of Genghis Khan. The khan died in August 1227, during the war against the Tangut people. To ensure the success of the Tangut campaign and to prevent uprisings in other parts of the empire, word of the khan's death was kept secret; every person who encountered the procession was killed. Genghis Khan was buried on Mount Burkan-Kaldun, but the exact location of his grave is unknown.

Above and left, views of the two unsuccessful Mongol invasions of Japan, mounted in 1274 and 1281. The first invasion force, of about 10,000 soldiers, was so poorly equipped that it lost a major battle when its supply of arrows ran out. The second invasion force, of some 140,000 men, was held to a narrow beachhead by the Japanese; after two months, its fleet of 3,500 ships was wrecked by a typhoon. The Japanese called the storm kamikaze—the divine wind—a word they used in World War Two to refer to their corps of suicide pilots. Right, a Japanese depiction of a Mongol archer and three horses.